Better Homes and Gardens®

New Casserole Cook Book

Our seal assures you that every recipe in the *New Casserole Cook Book*
has been tested in the Better Homes and Gardens® Test Kitchen.
This means that each recipe is practical and reliable, and
meets our high standards of taste appeal.

BETTER HOMES AND GARDENS® BOOKS

Editor: Gerald M. Knox
Art Director: Ernest Shelton
Managing Editor: David A. Kirchner
Editorial Project Managers: Liz Anderson, James D. Blume,
    Marsha Jahns, Rosanne Weber Mattson

Department Head, Cook Books: Sharyl Heiken
Associate Department Heads: Sandra Granseth,
    Rosemary C. Hutchinson, Elizabeth Woolever
Senior Food Editors: Linda Henry, Marcia Stanley,
    Joyce Trollope
Associate Food Editors: Mary Major, Diana McMillen,
    Mary Jo Plutt, Linda Foley Woodrum
Test Kitchen: Director, Sharon Stilwell; Photo Studio Director,
    Janet Herwig; Home Economists: Jean Brekke, Kay Cargill,
    Marilyn Cornelius, Jennifer Darling, Maryellyn Krantz,
    Lynelle Munn, Dianna Nolin, Marge Steenson

Associate Art Directors: Neoma Thomas, Linda Ford Vermie,
    Randall Yontz
Assistant Art Directors: Lynda Haupert, Harijs Priekulis,
    Tom Wegner
Graphic Designers: Mary Schlueter Bendgen, Mike Burns,
    Brian Wignall
Art Production: Director, John Berg; Associate, Joe Heuer;
    Office Manager, Michaela Lester

President, Book Group: Jeramy Lanigan
Vice President, Retail Marketing: Jamie L. Martin
Vice President, Administrative Services: Rick Rundall

BETTER HOMES AND GARDENS® MAGAZINE
President, Magazine Group: James A. Autry
Editorial Director: Doris Eby
Food and Nutrition Editor: Nancy Byal

MEREDITH CORPORATION OFFICERS
Chairman of the Executive Committee: E.T. Meredith III
Chairman of the Board: Robert A. Burnett
President: Jack D. Rehm

NEW CASSEROLE COOK BOOK

Editor: Mary Major
Editorial Project Manager: Rosanne Weber Mattson
Graphic Designer: Mary Schlueter Bendgen
Electronic Text Processor: Paula Forest
Food Stylists: Suzanne Finley, Janet Herwig
Contributing Photographers: Michael Jensen, Scott Little

On the cover: *Spanish Chicken Casserole*
(see recipe, page 7)

Contents

4 Dinner in a Dish

Discover the advantages of carefree casseroles.

6 Updated Casseroles

Easy-to-fix one-dish meals featuring tasty new combinations.

22 Mealtime Favorites

Tuna-noodle casserole, plus lots more.

38 Main-Dish Pies

Savory meat, poultry, and fish fillings with a crust.

48 Make-Ahead Casseroles

Fix and freeze a casserole to savor later.

58 Potluck Casseroles

Feed a bunch with these totable dinners.

66 Come for Brunch

Start your day with an eye-opening casserole.

74 Casseroles on the Side

Vegetable combos to serve alongside meat, poultry, or fish.

79 Index

Dinner in a Dish

Call them casseroles, one-dish meals, or hot dishes. By any name, they mean deliciously easy cooking. Whether you choose *Pepper and Beef Rolls* (shown at right) or any other main-dish recipe in the *New Casserole Cook Book,* there's no need to cook separate vegetable, pasta, or rice side dishes because they bake along with the meat in a flavorful sauce. Just add a dessert to complete your meal.

And while casseroles bake, the flavors of the different foods blend and meld together, producing a taste special to each recipe.

Take a look at the recipes we offer. Then, turn on your oven and start an easy one-dish oven meal.

Peppers =

**Pepper and
Beef Rolls**
(see recipe, page 28)

Updated Casseroles

For the latest word in casseroles look to these recipes that include today's favorite flavors and are easier to prepare than ever before. We've used ingredients you may not have thought of adding to a casserole. For example, many of our casseroles contain the Mexican and Oriental ingredients now readily available in grocery stores. Throughout, we've kept an eye on convenience, too, by using frozen vegetables, packaged mixes, and precooked meats. You'll also notice shorter cooking times and no unnecessary steps. Take a look at these recipes and you'll see casseroles in a new light.

Havarti Chicken Bake

2 tablespoons margarine *or* butter	● In a 2-quart saucepan melt margarine or butter. Stir in flour, salt, nutmeg, and pepper. Add milk all at once. Cook and stir over medium heat till mixture is thickened and bubbly. Add ½ *cup* of the cheese, stirring till melted. Stir in chicken or turkey, broccoli, and, if desired, almonds. Transfer to a 1½-quart casserole. Sprinkle with remaining cheese.
2 tablespoons all-purpose flour	
¼ teaspoon salt	
⅛ teaspoon ground nutmeg	
Dash pepper	
1 cup milk	
1 cup shredded havarti, Swiss, cheddar, *or* American cheese (4 ounces)	
1½ cups chopped cooked chicken *or* turkey	
1 10-ounce package frozen cut broccoli, thawed	
¼ cup slivered almonds, toasted (optional)	

Choose your cheese, as you please. Havarti, Swiss, cheddar, or American cheese taste equally good in this dish.

1 beaten egg	● In a small mixing bowl combine egg, flour, milk, oil, and salt. Beat with a rotary beater till smooth. Pour egg mixture over chicken mixture. Bake, uncovered, in a 425° oven for 25 to 30 minutes or till golden brown. Serves 4.
½ cup all-purpose flour	
½ cup milk	
2 teaspoons cooking oil	
⅛ teaspoon salt	

Spanish Chicken Casserole

2	whole chicken breasts, split
2	tablespoons cooking oil
1	medium onion, chopped
¼	cup chopped green pepper
1	clove garlic, minced
1	tablespoon chili powder
⅛	teaspoon ground cinnamon
⅛	teaspoon ground cumin

● Remove skin from chicken, if desired. In a large skillet cook chicken in hot oil till brown on both sides. Remove chicken from skillet. Add onion, green pepper, garlic, chili powder, cinnamon, cumin, and ⅛ teaspoon *pepper*. Cook till vegetables are tender. Drain excess fat from the skillet.

Pictured on the cover.

No peeking! Keep this Mexican-style dish covered with foil during the first 35 minutes so the rice cooks and the chicken stays moist.

1	16-ounce can tomatoes, cut up
1	cup water
¾	cup long grain rice
2	teaspoons instant chicken bouillon granules
½	cup picante sauce
½	cup shredded cheddar cheese (2 ounces)
	Sliced pitted ripe olives

● Stir in *undrained* tomatoes, water, rice, and chicken bouillon granules. Bring to boiling. Turn rice mixture into a 12x7½x2-inch baking dish. Arrange chicken on top.
    Bake, covered, in a 350° oven for 35 minutes. Spoon picante sauce over chicken. Sprinkle with cheese. Bake, uncovered, 5 minutes longer or till chicken is tender. Sprinkle with olives. Makes 4 servings.

Easy Bratwurst Bake

1	cup medium noodles
2	cups loose-pack frozen zucchini, carrots, cauliflower, lima beans, and Italian beans
1	pound smoked fully cooked bratwurst

● Cook noodles according to package directions, adding frozen vegetables the last 5 minutes. Drain. Meanwhile, cut the sausage into ½-inch pieces.

Substitute any fully cooked link sausage for the bratwurst. If you buy uncooked sausage, just cook it before adding it to the casserole.

1	12-ounce jar mushroom *or* chicken gravy
½	teaspoon dried sage, crushed

● In a 2-quart casserole combine gravy, sage, noodle mixture, and sausage. Mix well. Bake, covered, in a 350° oven for 25 to 30 minutes or till heated through. Makes 4 servings.

Microwave Directions: Cook the noodles according to package directions, adding frozen vegetables for the last 5 minutes. Drain. In a 2-quart microwave-safe casserole combine gravy, sage, noodle mixture, and sausage. Micro-cook, covered, on 100% power (high) for 6 to 8 minutes or till heated through, stirring after 4 minutes.

Turkey Alfredo Casserole

6 ounces fettuccine *or* medium noodles 1 10-ounce package frozen cut broccoli	● Cook pasta according to package directions. Drain and set aside. Run water over broccoli to thaw.
3 tablespoons margarine *or* butter 3 tablespoons all-purpose flour ½ teaspoon dried basil, crushed ¼ teaspoon salt ⅛ teaspoon pepper 2½ cups milk 2½ cups chopped cooked turkey *or* chicken ½ cup grated Parmesan cheese	● For sauce, in a large saucepan melt margarine or butter. Stir in flour, basil, salt, and pepper. Add milk all at once. Cook and stir till thickened and bubbly. Cook and stir for 1 minute more. Remove from heat. Stir in turkey or chicken, Parmesan cheese, and broccoli. Remove from heat. Add pasta and toss to coat.
¼ cup grated Pamesan cheese Carrot curls (optional)	● Turn turkey mixture into a greased 12x7½x2-inch baking dish. Cover with foil. Bake in a 350° oven for 20 minutes. Remove foil. Sprinkle with Parmesan cheese. Bake, uncovered, for 5 to 10 minutes more or till heated through. Garnish with carrot curls, if desired. Makes 4 servings.

Toss some turkey and broccoli flowerets with fettuccine Alfredo for an updated turkey-noodle casserole.

Microwave Directions: Cook pasta according to package directions. In a 2-quart microwave-safe casserole micro-cook frozen broccoli according to package directions. Drain and set aside.

For sauce, in the 2-quart casserole cook margarine or butter on 100% power (high) for 50 to 60 seconds or till melted. Stir in flour, basil, salt, and pepper. Add milk all at once. Cook, uncovered, on high for 6 to 9 minutes or till thickened and bubbly, stirring every minute. Cook, uncovered, for 30 seconds more. Stir in turkey or chicken, ½ cup grated Parmesan cheese, and broccoli. Add pasta and toss to coat.

Cook, covered, on high for 5 to 7 minutes or till heated through, stirring once. Sprinkle with ¼ cup grated Parmesan cheese. Top with carrot curls, if desired.

Orange Chicken With Rice

2 whole medium chicken
   breasts (1½ pounds
   total), skinned, boned,
   and halved lengthwise
2 tablespoons cooking oil

● Cut chicken into 1-inch pieces. In a large skillet cook half the chicken in hot oil till no longer pink, stirring constantly. Remove chicken. Repeat with remaining chicken. Return all chicken to skillet.

Sometimes casseroles go together more easily when you combine cooking methods. In this recipe, try micro-cooking the chicken, and then switching to the conventional method to bake the casserole.

1½ cups sliced fresh
    mushrooms
1½ cups frozen crinkle-cut
    carrots
1½ cups water
 ¾ cup long grain rice
 ½ of a 6-ounce can (⅓ cup)
    frozen orange juice
    concentrate
 ¼ cup soy sauce
 ⅛ teaspoon garlic powder
 ⅛ teaspoon pepper

● Stir in mushrooms, carrots, water, rice, orange juice concentrate, soy sauce, garlic powder, and pepper. Bring to boiling. Turn mixture into a 2-quart casserole.

Bake, covered, in a 350° oven about 35 minutes or till rice is tender. Serves 4.

Microwave Directions: Omit cooking oil. Substitute 1¼ cups *quick-cooking rice* for the long grain rice. Reduce water to ¾ cup.

Cut the chicken into 1-inch pieces. In a 2-quart microwave-safe casserole micro-cook chicken, covered, on 100% power (high) for 5 to 7 minutes or till no longer pink, stirring once. Remove chicken. Drain excess liquid.

In the same casserole combine mushrooms and carrots. Cook, covered, on high for 3 to 4 minutes or till tender, stirring once. Stir in 1¼ cups *quick-cooking rice,* ¾ cup water, orange juice concentrate, soy sauce, garlic powder, pepper, and chicken.

Cook, covered, on high for 6 to 8 minutes or till hot and bubbly, stirring once. Let stand, covered, for 5 minutes.

Chicken and Green Beans Parmesan

1 **9-ounce package frozen Italian-style** *or* **cut green beans**	● Run water over green beans to separate. In an 8x8x2-inch baking dish stir together beans, ¾ *cup* of the spaghetti sauce, Parmesan cheese, and red pepper. Arrange chicken over the bean mixture. Drizzle with remaining spaghetti sauce.
1 **cup meatless spaghetti sauce**	
3 **tablespoons grated Parmesan cheese**	
⅛ **teaspoon ground red pepper**	
2 **whole small chicken breasts (about 1 pound total), skinned, boned, and halved lengthwise**	
½ **cup shredded mozzarella cheese (2 ounces)**	● Bake, covered, in a 350° oven for 40 to 45 minutes or till chicken and beans are tender. Sprinkle with mozzarella cheese. Bake about 2 minutes more or till cheese melts. Makes 4 servings.

This quick-to-go-together casserole requires no precooking of the chicken or beans.

Microwave Directions: Run water over green beans to separate. In an 8x8x2-inch microwave-safe baking dish combine beans, ¾ *cup* spaghetti sauce, Parmesan cheese, and red pepper. Cover with vented microwave-safe plastic wrap.

Micro-cook on 100% power (high) for 5 minutes. Stir. Arrange chicken over bean mixture. Drizzle with remaining sauce. Cook, covered, on high for 7 to 8 minutes more or till chicken is no longer pink, giving dish a half-turn once. Sprinkle with mozzarella cheese. Cook, uncovered, on high for 30 to 60 seconds more or till the cheese melts.

Salmon-Potato Bake

1 **5.5-ounce package dry au gratin potato mix**	● In a 2-quart casserole prepare potatoes according to package directions for oven method, *except* omit margarine or butter. Stir in salmon, frozen peas, and dillweed.
1 **15½-ounce can salmon, drained, broken into chunks, and skin and bones removed**	
1 **cup frozen peas**	Bake, covered, in a 400° oven for 30 to 35 minutes or till potatoes are tender. Makes 4 or 5 servings.
½ **teaspoon dried dillweed**	

You're only a few ingredients away from mealtime with this convenient off-the-shelf casserole.

Thanksgiving-In-a-Dish

1 **18-ounce can sweet potatoes, drained**
1 **egg**
¼ **cup orange juice**
¼ **teaspoon ground cinnamon**
2 **cups chopped cooked turkey *or* chicken**

● In a large mixer bowl combine sweet potatoes, egg, orange juice, and cinnamon. Beat with an electric mixer on medium speed till smooth. Stir in turkey or chicken. Spoon mixture into four 10-ounce individual casseroles (or one 1-quart casserole).
    Bake, uncovered, in a 375° oven about 25 minutes (45 minutes for 1-quart casserole) or till heated through.

Pull out the traditional Thanksgiving ingredients—turkey, sweet potatoes, and cranberry sauce—for an easy supper.

1 **8-ounce can whole cranberry sauce**
1 **teaspoon finely shredded orange peel**

● Meanwhile, in a small saucepan stir together cranberry sauce and orange peel. Heat through. Serve with casseroles. Makes 4 servings.

Turkey and Broccoli Bake

1 **10-ounce package frozen broccoli spears**
12 **ounces sliced cooked turkey breast**
1 **10½-ounce can chicken gravy**

● Cook broccoli spears according to package directions, *except* omit salt. Drain broccoli and set aside.
    In four 10-ounce casseroles or au gratin dishes arrange turkey slices. Place broccoli spears over turkey. Reserve ¼ cup of the gravy. Divide remaining gravy among the casseroles.

Use sliced turkey from the deli or buy a cooked turkey breast portion and slice it yourself.

¼ **cup chopped onion**
¼ **cup chopped celery**
1 **tablespoon margarine *or* butter**
1 **cup herb-seasoned croutons**

● In a small skillet cook onion and celery in margarine or butter till tender. Stir in croutons and reserved gravy. Spoon crouton mixture down the center of each casserole.
    Bake in a 350° oven for 30 to 35 minutes or till heated through. Makes 4 servings.

Turkey Meatball Stew

1 **beaten egg**	● In a medium mixing bowl combine egg, bread crumbs, milk, minced onion, parsley flakes, pepper, salt, and sage. Add ground turkey. Mix well. Shape into 1-inch meatballs.
1 **cup soft bread crumbs (1½ slices)**	
3 **tablespoons milk**	
1 **tablespoon dried minced onion**	
1 **tablespoon dried parsley flakes**	Arrange meatballs in a shallow baking pan. Bake in a 375° oven about 15 minutes or till no longer pink.
½ **teaspoon pepper**	
¼ **teaspoon salt**	
¼ **teaspoon ground sage**	
1 **pound ground raw turkey**	

1 **cup frozen small whole onions**	● Meanwhile, run onions under cold water to thaw. In a 2-quart casserole combine sweet potatoes, gravy, orange peel, and onions. Gently stir in meatballs.
1 **18-ounce can sweet potatoes, drained and cut into 1-inch pieces**	
1 **12-ounce jar chicken gravy**	Bake, covered, in a 375° oven for 35 to 40 minutes or till onions are tender. Makes 4 servings.
½ **teaspoon finely shredded orange peel**	

Baking the meatballs in the oven rather than browning them in a skillet means they can cook unattended.

Cheesy Rice Bake

1 **cup long grain rice**	● Cook the rice according to package directions.

1 **8-ounce carton dairy sour cream**	● In a large mixing bowl stir together sour cream and red pepper. Stir in cheese, chili peppers, pimiento, and cooked rice. Mix well. Turn into an 8-inch round baking dish.
⅛ **teaspoon ground red pepper**	
2 **cups shredded cheddar *or* Monterey Jack cheese (8 ounces)**	
1 **4-ounce can diced green chili peppers, drained**	Bake, covered, in a 350° oven for 30 to 35 minutes or till heated through. Sprinkle with chips and green onions. Makes 4 servings.
1 **2-ounce jar diced pimiento, drained**	
½ **cup coarsely crushed tortilla *or* corn chips**	
2 **green onions, sliced**	

We put enough cheese in this casserole for a satisfying main dish. To make it a side dish, double the number of servings.

Mexican Turkey Casserole

1½ **cups chopped cooked turkey** *or* **chicken**
1 **12-ounce jar chicken gravy**
1 **8-ounce carton dairy sour cream**
1 **4-ounce can diced green chili peppers, drained**
2 **green onions, sliced**
2 **tablespoons sliced pitted ripe olives**

● In a large mixing bowl combine the turkey or chicken, gravy, sour cream, chili peppers, green onions, and olives.

1½ **cups coarsely crushed corn chips**
1½ **cups shredded cheddar** *and/or* **Monterey Jack cheese (6 ounces)**
1 **cherry tomato, cut in half (optional)**
   Parsley sprigs (optional)
1 **large tomato, chopped**
   Shredded lettuce

● Grease the sides of a 1½-quart casserole. Sprinkle a *third* of the corn chips over the bottom of casserole. Pour *half* of the turkey mixture over chips. Top with *half* of the cheese. Repeat layers, ending with a layer of chips.

Bake in a 375° oven about 35 minutes or till heated through. Garnish with cherry tomato and parsley, if desired. Serve with chopped tomato and lettuce. Makes 4 or 5 servings.

Microwave Directions: In a 1½-quart microwave-safe casserole prepare as above, *except* reserve the last ½ cup corn chips. Micro-cook, covered, on 100% power (high) for 9 to 12 minutes or till heated through, stirring once. Top with reserved corn chips. Serve as above.

Shrimp and Rice au Gratin

1 11-ounce can condensed cheddar cheese soup
1 8-ounce package frozen peeled and deveined shrimp, thawed and drained, *or* one 12-ounce can skinless, boneless salmon, drained and flaked
1 cup quick-cooking rice
1 cup milk
1 4-ounce can sliced mushrooms, drained
2 green onions, thinly sliced
2 tablespoons dry sherry (optional)

● In a 1½-quart casserole combine soup, shrimp or salmon, rice, milk, mushrooms, green onions, and, if desired, sherry. Mix well.

Bake, covered, in a 350° oven for 35 to 40 minutes or till the rice is almost tender and mixture is hot. Stir.

Cheddar cheese soup imparts the traditional "au gratin" flavor to this dish. Give it a Mexican flavor by substituting a can of nacho cheese soup.

¼ cup fine dry bread crumbs
2 tablespoons margarine *or* butter, melted
1 tablespoon grated Parmesan cheese

● Meanwhile, in a small bowl combine bread crumbs, margarine or butter, and Parmesan cheese. Sprinkle over shrimp mixture. Bake, uncovered, about 10 minutes more or till the topping is golden. Makes 4 servings.

Microwave Directions: If using shrimp, *decrease* milk to ¾ cup. In a 1½-quart microwave-safe casserole combine soup, shrimp or salmon, rice, milk, mushrooms, onion, and, if desired, sherry. Micro-cook, covered, on 100% power (high) for 7 to 9 minutes or till mixture is hot and bubbly and shrimp turn pink, stirring once. Let stand, covered, for 5 minutes.

Meanwhile, combine bread crumbs, margarine or butter, and Parmesan cheese. Sprinkle crumb mixture over casserole before serving.

Attention, Microwave Owners

We tested all our recipes in countertop microwave ovens that have 600 to 700 watts of cooking power. Cooking times are approximate since microwave ovens vary by manufacturer.

Oriental Beef Bake

12 ounces sliced cooked beef,
cut into julienne strips
(about 2¼ cups)
1 15¼-ounce can pineapple
chunks
1 12-ounce jar mushroom
gravy
1 cup quick-cooking rice
4 green onions, cut into
1-inch pieces
1 8-ounce can sliced water
chestnuts, drained
1 4-ounce can sliced
mushrooms, drained
1 2-ounce jar sliced
pimiento, drained
2 tablespoons soy sauce
½ teaspoon ground ginger

● In a 2-quart casserole combine beef, *undrained* pineapple, gravy, rice, green onions, water chestnuts, mushrooms, pimiento, soy sauce, and ginger.

Bake, covered, in a 375° oven for 35 to 40 minutes or till rice is tender, stirring once. Serve with additional soy sauce, if desired. Makes 4 or 5 servings.

Sliced roast beef from the deli makes this easy stir-and-bake casserole even easier.

Microwave Directions: In a 2-quart microwave-safe casserole combine beef, *undrained* pineapple, gravy, rice, green onions, water chestnuts, mushrooms, pimiento, soy sauce, and ginger.

Micro-cook, covered, on 100% power (high) for 10 to 12 minutes or till hot and bubbly, stirring once. Let stand, covered, for 5 minutes before serving.

Easy Cheesy Fish Bake

1 pound fresh *or* frozen
skinless orange roughy,
catfish, pike, cod, *or*
haddock fish fillets
(½ to ¾ inch thick)

● Thaw fish, if frozen. Cut fillets into 1-inch pieces.

For a munchy, crunchy topping, sprinkle some toasted pecans or almonds over the casserole for the last few minutes of baking.

1 8-ounce jar cheese spread
¼ cup milk
1 10-ounce package frozen
peas
1 cup quick-cooking rice
⅛ teaspoon dried dillweed

● In a 1½-quart casserole stir together cheese spread and milk (mixture will be lumpy). Stir in peas, rice, dillweed, and fish. Bake, covered, in a 375° oven for 40 to 45 minutes or till heated through, stirring once or twice. Makes 4 servings.

Flounder and Spinach Bake

1 pound fresh *or* frozen
   flounder *or* sole fillets
1 10-ounce package frozen
   chopped spinach,
   thawed and well drained
1½ cups seasoned croutons,
   coarsely crushed
1 8-ounce can whole kernel
   corn, drained
¾ cup shredded Swiss cheese
   (3 ounces)
1 beaten egg
3 tablespoons water
   Salt
   Lemon pepper *or* pepper

● Thaw fish fillets, if frozen. Combine spinach, croutons, corn, and cheese. Combine egg and water. Add to spinach mixture; mix well.

Spread spinach mixture evenly in a 12x7½x2-inch baking dish. Cover with foil. Bake in a 375° oven for 10 minutes. Arrange fish fillets over spinach mixture, overlapping if necessary. Sprinkle with salt and lemon pepper or pepper.

Popeye tries to include spinach in everything he eats. Here, he gives an approving wink to this fish and spinach casserole.

1 medium tomato, cut into
   12 thin wedges
¼ cup shredded Swiss cheese
   (1 ounce)

● Cover with foil. Bake for 15 minutes. Remove foil. Arrange tomato wedges on fillets. Sprinkle with cheese. Bake about 5 minutes more or till fish flakes easily with a fork. Makes 6 servings.

Microwave Directions: Thaw fish fillets, if frozen. Prepare spinach mixture as directed above. Spread mixture in a 12x7½x2-inch microwave-safe baking dish. Cover with vented microwave-safe plastic wrap. Micro-cook on 100% power (high) for 3 minutes. Arrange fish fillets over spinach mixture. Cook, covered, on high for 3 minutes. Arrange tomato wedges on fillets. Sprinkle with ¼ cup cheese. Cook, covered, on high for 1½ to 2½ minutes or till fish flakes easily with a fork.

Chicken Chow Mein Bake

½ cup mayonnaise *or* salad dressing
2 green onions, sliced
1 tablespoon all-purpose flour
1 tablespoon soy sauce
2 cups chopped cooked turkey *or* chicken
1 16-ounce can fancy mixed Chinese vegetables, drained

● In a 1-quart casserole combine mayonnaise or salad dressing, green onions, flour, and soy sauce. Fold in chicken and vegetables.

Presto! This casserole turns into a hot chicken salad when you serve it on a bed of shredded lettuce.

½ cup chow mein noodles

● Bake, covered, in a 350° oven about 30 minutes or till heated through. Sprinkle with chow mein noodles. Bake, uncovered, 5 minutes more. Serves 4.

If the Dish Fits . . .

Some recipes call for a casserole and some call for a baking dish. The difference may be slight, but the right dish contributes to the success of your recipe.

A casserole is round or oval. To determine the volume of the casserole, measure the amount of water it holds when filled completely to the top. Casseroles often come with their own fitted lid.

A baking dish is square or rectangular and about 2 inches deep. To determine the size of a baking dish, measure across the top from the inside edges. You can use foil when the recipe specifies a cover.

For best results, use the casserole or baking dish specified in a recipe. The food bubbles over if the dish is too small and dries out if it's too big.

Salmon Soufflé

¼ cup margarine *or* butter
¼ cup all-purpose flour
½ teaspoon dried marjoram, crushed
1 cup milk
1 7¾-ounce can salmon, drained, flaked, and skin and bones removed
½ cup shredded cheddar cheese (2 ounces)
1 tablespoon Worcestershire sauce
4 egg yolks

● In a medium saucepan melt margarine or butter. Stir in flour, marjoram, ¼ teaspoon *salt*, and ⅛ teaspoon *pepper*. Add milk all at once. Cook and stir over medium heat till thickened and bubbly. Cook and stir for 1 minute more.
Stir salmon, cheddar cheese, and Worcestershire sauce into milk mixture. Cook and stir till cheese melts. Remove from heat. Beat egg yolks with a fork till combined. Gradually add salmon mixture to yolks, stirring constantly. Set aside.

4 egg whites

● Using clean beaters, beat egg whites till stiff peaks form (tips stand straight). Stir ½ cup beaten whites into salmon-yolk mixture. Gradually pour salmon-yolk mixture over remaining whites, folding to combine. Pour into ungreased 1½-quart soufflé dish with a foil collar.
Bake in a 350° oven about 40 minutes or till a knife inserted near center comes out clean. Serve immediately. Makes 4 servings.

A soufflé needs room to "grow," so we suggest making a foil collar. Start with a 12-inch-wide sheet of foil, long enough to go around the dish and overlap by 2 inches. Fold the foil horizontally in thirds. Wrap the collar around the dish and fasten it with paper clips. The collar should extend 2 to 3 inches above the rim of the dish.

Spicy Louisiana Chicken Bake

1 16-ounce can tomatoes, cut up
1 cup tomato juice
⅔ cup long grain rice
1 medium onion, chopped
½ cup chopped celery
½ cup chopped green pepper
2 teaspoons instant chicken bouillon granules
¼ teaspoon garlic powder
⅛ to ¼ teaspoon ground red pepper

● In a 13x9x2-inch baking dish stir together *undrained* tomatoes, tomato juice, rice, onion, celery, green pepper, chicken bouillon granules, garlic powder, and red pepper.

2½ pounds meaty chicken pieces (breasts, thighs, and drumsticks)
Paprika

● Remove skin from chicken, if desired. Arrange the chicken pieces on top of the rice mixture. Sprinkle chicken with paprika. Cover with foil.
Bake in a 375° oven for 50 to 60 minutes or till chicken and rice are tender. Makes 6 servings.

Our spunky chicken and rice casserole deserves some authentic Louisiana fixin's. Either fresh or frozen okra does the trick.

Mealtime Favorites

Some foods naturally go together, such as chicken and rice or pork chops and cabbage. These recipes take combinations like those one step further by cooking them together as delicious one-dish meals. Look for your favorite casseroles, such as *Macaroni and Cheese* and *Chicken Tetrazzini.* Each recipe features home-style cooking at its best.

Pork Chops With Scalloped Potatoes

4 pork chops, cut ½ inch thick
1 tablespoon cooking oil
1 10¾-ounce can condensed cream of celery soup
1 cup milk
3 green onions, sliced

● In a large skillet cook the pork chops in hot oil till brown on both sides. Remove chops from skillet. Drain on paper towels. Drain fat from skillet and wipe dry. In skillet combine soup, milk, and green onions. Cook till heated through. Remove from heat.

3 medium potatoes, sliced ¼ inch thick (3 cups)
4 slices American cheese (4 ounces)
⅛ teaspoon pepper

● In an 8x8x2-inch baking dish arrange *half* of the potatoes. Top with cheese slices and then remaining potatoes. Place pork chops on top of potatoes. Sprinkle chops with pepper. Pour soup mixture over chops and potatoes. Cover with foil. Bake in a 350° oven for 1¼ hours. Remove foil. Bake about 30 minutes more or till pork chops and potatoes are tender. Makes 4 servings.

When browning chops for casseroles like *Pork Chops with Scalloped Potatoes,* heat the oil first. Then add the chops and cook over medium heat till brown on one side, about 5 minutes. Finally, turn and cook another 5 minutes or till the other side browns.

Lamb-Vegetable Stew

1 pound boneless lamb, cut into ¾-inch cubes	● In a large skillet cook lamb cubes in hot oil till brown. Stir in flour, salt, thyme, and pepper. Add water and Worcestershire sauce all at once. Cook and stir till thickened and bubbly. Cook and stir for 1 minute more.
2 tablespoons cooking oil	
¼ cup all-purpose flour	
¾ teaspoon salt	
½ teaspoon dried thyme, crushed	
¼ teaspoon pepper	
2 cups hot water	
1 teaspoon Worcestershire sauce	

The sweet, mellow flavor of turnips blends with lamb in this country-style oven stew.

2 medium turnips, peeled and chopped (2 cups)	● In a 2-quart casserole combine turnips, potato, carrots, onion, parsley, and lamb mixture.
1 large potato, peeled and sliced (1½ cups)	Bake, covered, in a 350° oven for 1¼ to 1½ hours or till meat and vegetables are tender, stirring occasionally. Sprinkle with additional snipped parsley, if desired. Makes 4 servings.
2 medium carrots, sliced (1 cup)	
1 medium onion, cut into thin wedges	
¼ cup snipped parsley	

Pork Chop And Cabbage Dinner

4 pork chops, cut ¾ inch thick	● In a 12-inch oven proof skillet cook pork chops in hot oil till brown on both sides. Remove chops from skillet. Add onion. Cook till tender.
1 tablespoon cooking oil	
1 medium onion, sliced	

If your skillet has a wooden or plastic handle, cover the handle with foil before baking. Or, transfer the entire mixture to a 13x9x2-inch baking dish.

½ cup dry white wine	● Stir in wine, brown sugar, vinegar, salt, and pepper. Stir in cabbage and apples. Bring mixture to boiling. Top with chops. Cover and bake in a 350° oven for 40 to 45 minutes or till pork chops are tender. Makes 4 servings.
¼ cup packed brown sugar	
1 tablespoon white wine vinegar	
1 teaspoon salt	
¼ teaspoon pepper	
4 cups shredded cabbage	
2 large cooking apples, cored and thinly sliced	

Pastitsio

8 ounces cut ziti *or* elbow macaroni	● Cook pasta according to package directions. Drain well.
1 pound ground lamb *or* beef 1 medium onion, chopped (½ cup) 1 clove garlic, minced 1 15-ounce can tomato sauce ½ teaspoon dried oregano, crushed ¼ teaspoon ground cinnamon ¼ teaspoon pepper ¾ cup grated Parmesan cheese	● Meanwhile, in a large skillet cook lamb or beef, onion, and garlic till the meat is brown. Drain fat from skillet. Stir in tomato sauce, oregano, cinnamon, and pepper. Cook, covered, about 5 minutes or till heated through. Remove from heat. Stir in cheese. 　Layer *half* of the pasta in an 8x8x2-inch baking dish. Top with meat mixture, then the remaining pasta.
2 tablespoons margarine *or* butter 2 tablespoons all-purpose flour ⅛ teaspoon pepper 1½ cups milk 1 beaten egg ¼ cup grated Parmesan cheese	● For the sauce, in a small saucepan melt margarine or butter. Stir in flour and pepper till blended. Add milk all at once. Cook and stir over medium heat till mixture is thickened and bubbly. Stir some of the mixture into the beaten egg. Return egg mixture to saucepan. Cook and stir for 2 minutes more. Stir in Parmesan cheese. 　Pour sauce over the pasta layer. Bake, uncovered, in a 350° oven about 35 minutes or till heated through. Sprinkle with additional Parmesan cheese, if desired. Let stand 10 minutes before serving. Makes 6 servings.

Greeks love this layered lamb and pasta casserole. They serve it for any occasion from a casual family gathering to a special anniversary.

Macaroni And Cheese

1½ cups elbow macaroni (6 ounces) ¼ cup finely chopped onion 3 tablespoons margarine *or* butter 2 tablespoons all-purpose flour ¼ teaspoon salt 2½ cups milk 2 cups cubed American cheese (8 ounces)	● Cook macaroni according to package directions. Drain. 　For cheese sauce, in a large saucepan cook onion in margarine or butter till tender but not brown. Stir in the flour, salt, and dash *pepper*. Add milk all at once. Cook and stir till thickened and bubbly. Add cubed cheese; stir till melted.
1 medium tomato, sliced	● Stir macaroni into sauce. Turn into a 1½-quart casserole. Bake in a 350° oven for 20 minutes. Arrange tomato slices on top. Bake for 5 to 10 minutes more or till heated through. Makes 4 main-dish servings or 8 side-dish servings.

This all-American favorite calls out for American cheese. Because it contains plenty, serve it for the main course.

Pastitsio

Knockwurst, Apples, and Sauerkraut

1 **pound knockwurst** *or* **frankfurters, cut into 1-inch pieces**
1 **14-ounce can sauerkraut, rinsed and drained**
2 **medium apples, cored and chopped**
⅓ **cup apple juice**
1 **teaspoon caraway seed**

● In a 2-quart casserole combine knockwurst or frankfurters, sauerkraut, apples, apple juice, and caraway seed. Bake, covered, in a 350° oven for 30 to 35 minutes or till heated through. Makes 4 servings.

Baking this popular trio in a casserole makes an easy, no-fuss supper.

Microwave Directions: In a 2-quart microwave-safe casserole combine knockwurst or frankfurters, sauerkraut, apples, apple juice, and caraway seed. Micro-cook, covered, on 100% power (high) for 8 to 10 minutes or till heated through, stirring after 4 minutes.

Chicken and Rice in a Dish

1 **10¾-ounce can condensed cream of mushroom soup** *or* **condensed cream of chicken soup**
½ **cup dairy sour cream**
½ **cup milk**
1 **teaspoon dried basil, crushed**
1 **cup quick-cooking rice**

● Combine soup, sour cream, milk, and basil. Measure ½ *cup* of the soup mixture; set aside. Combine remaining soup mixture and rice. Spread in the bottom of a 12x7½x2-inch baking dish.

To save time and effort, purchase boneless chicken breasts for this easy-to-assemble dish.

1 **10-ounce package frozen broccoli spears**
2 **whole chicken breasts, skinned, boned, and halved lengthwise**
½ **cup shredded Swiss cheese (2 ounces)**

● Rinse broccoli spears with water to separate. Drain. Arrange broccoli spears and chicken over rice mixture. Spoon reserved sauce over all. Cover with foil.
   Bake in a 350° oven for 50 to 60 minutes or till chicken and rice are tender. Sprinkle with cheese. Serves 4.

Coq au Vin

2 slices bacon
2 to 2½ pounds meaty
   chicken pieces (breasts,
   thighs, and drumsticks)

● In a large skillet cook bacon till crisp. Remove bacon, reserving drippings. Drain on paper towels. Crumble bacon.
   Remove the skin from the chicken pieces. Cook chicken in bacon drippings about 15 minutes or till brown, turning chicken as necessary. Transfer chicken to a 3-quart casserole. Drain skillet, reserving 2 tablespoons drippings.

We simplified this classic French dish with frozen vegetables, instant chicken bouillon, and no-watch oven cooking.

3 tablespoons all-purpose
   flour
1 bay leaf
1 teaspoon instant chicken
   bouillon granules
½ teaspoon dried marjoram,
   crushed
½ teaspoon dried thyme,
   crushed
¼ teaspoon pepper
¾ cup burgundy
½ cup water

● Stir flour into reserved drippings. Add bay leaf, chicken bouillon granules, marjoram, thyme, and pepper. Stir in burgundy and water all at once. Cook and stir till thickened and bubbly. Cook and stir for 1 minute more.

1 10-ounce package frozen
   tiny whole carrots
1½ cups fresh small whole
   mushrooms
1 cup frozen small whole
   onions
2 tablespoons snipped
   parsley

● Stir in carrots, mushrooms, and onions. Heat to boiling. Pour over chicken. Bake, covered, in a 350° oven about 45 minutes or till chicken and vegetables are tender. Remove bay leaf. Sprinkle with parsley and crumbled bacon. Makes 6 servings.

Easy Oven Stew

1 pound beef stew meat, cut
   into ½-inch cubes
1 12-ounce jar brown gravy
1 6-ounce can tomato juice
   or vegetable juice
   cocktail
1 teaspoon dried basil,
   crushed
Dash pepper

● In a 2-quart casserole combine beef, gravy, tomato juice, basil, and pepper. Bake, covered, in a 350° oven for 45 minutes, stirring once.

Short on ingredients but long on flavor! A jar of gravy and a package of frozen mixed vegetables shorten the shopping list for this dish.

1 16- *or* 20-ounce package
   frozen vegetables for
   stew

● Stir in frozen vegetables. Bake, covered, for 1 to 1¼ hours more or till beef and vegetables are tender, stirring occasionally. Makes 4 servings.

Pepper and Beef Rolls

6 ounces medium noodles 1½ pounds beef round steak, cut ¾ inch thick	● Cook noodles according to package directions. Drain and set aside. Cut the steak into 6 pieces. Pound each with a meat mallet till about ¼ inch thick. Season with salt and pepper.
½ cup snipped parsley 1 medium sweet red *or* green pepper, cut into strips 2 tablespoons cooking oil	● Sprinkle each piece of meat with parsley. Place 2 or 3 pepper strips, crosswise, on each piece. Roll up the meat around the pepper strips. Secure with wooden toothpicks. In a large skillet cook the beef rolls in hot oil till brown on all sides. Remove from heat and set aside.
1 15½-ounce jar meatless spaghetti sauce 1 teaspoon dried oregano, crushed ¼ teaspoon garlic powder 2 tablespoons grated Parmesan cheese	● Combine spaghetti sauce, oregano, and garlic powder. Toss noodles with *1½ cups* of the sauce mixture. Turn into a greased 12x7½x2-inch baking dish. Arrange meat rolls on top. Spoon remaining sauce over the meat rolls. Sprinkle with Parmesan cheese. Cover with foil. Bake in a 350° oven for 45 to 50 minutes or till the meat is tender. Makes 6 servings.

Pictured on pages 4–5.

For extra color, use half of a red and half of a green pepper.

Pound the round steak with a meat mallet till it's about ¼ inch thick. Start at the center and work toward the outside edge.

Wrap the steak around the parsley and pepper strips. Fasten with a wooden toothpick to hold it together.

Chicken Tetrazzini

6 ounces spaghetti, broken 3 tablespoons margarine *or* butter 1½ cups sliced fresh mushrooms ¼ cup chopped green pepper	● Cook spaghetti according to package directions. Drain and set aside. 　Meanwhile, in a large saucepan melt margarine or butter. Add mushrooms and green pepper. Cook till tender.
¼ cup all-purpose flour ¼ teaspoon salt 1½ cups light cream *or* milk 1 cup chicken broth 2½ cups chopped cooked chicken *or* turkey 2 tablespoons dry sherry (optional)	● Stir flour and salt into mushroom mixture. Add light cream or milk and broth all at once. Cook and stir till thickened and bubbly. Stir in chicken or turkey and, if desired, sherry. Add spaghetti; toss to coat.
¼ cup grated Parmesan cheese ¼ cup sliced almonds	● Turn into a 12x7½x2-inch baking dish. Sprinkle with Parmesan cheese and sliced almonds. Bake in a 350° oven for 20 to 25 minutes or till heated through. Makes 5 or 6 servings.

Microwave Directions: Reduce light cream or milk to 1¼ cups. Cook spaghetti as directed above; drain. In a 2-quart microwave-safe casserole micro-cook margarine or butter on 100% power (high) for 40 to 50 seconds or till melted. Add mushrooms and green pepper. Cook, covered, on high for 2 to 3 minutes or till tender.

　Stir in flour, salt, 1¼ cups cream, and broth. Cook, uncovered, on high for 7 to 9 minutes or till thickened and bubbly, stirring every minute till slightly thickened, then every 30 seconds. Stir in chicken or turkey and, if desired, sherry. Add spaghetti; toss to coat.

　Cook, covered, on high for 5 to 7 minutes or till heated through, giving the dish a half-turn and stirring once. Sprinkle with Parmesan cheese and almonds before serving.

Tetrazzini, a popular combination of poultry, pasta, cream sauce, and cheese, first appeared in San Francisco and was named in honor of a famous opera singer, Luisa Tetrazzini.

Mom's Tuna-Noodle Casserole

4 ounces medium noodles

● Cook noodles according to package directions. Drain and set aside.

1 medium onion, finely chopped (½ cup)
½ cup finely chopped celery
2 tablespoons margarine *or* butter
1 10¾-ounce can condensed cream of mushroom soup
¾ cup milk
1 9¼-ounce can tuna, drained and flaked
1 cup frozen peas *or* peas and carrots *or* one 8-ounce can peas *or* peas and carrots, drained
¼ cup chopped pimiento
¼ cup grated Parmesan cheese

● In a medium saucepan cook onion and celery in margarine or butter till tender. Stir in soup and milk. Gently stir in tuna, peas, and pimiento. Toss tuna mixture with noodles. Turn into a 2-quart casserole. Sprinkle with cheese.
    Bake, uncovered, in a 375° oven for 30 to 35 minutes or till heated through. Makes 6 servings.

How do you improve on Mom's cooking? In this case, you don't. Her tuna casserole tastes as good today as it did 30 years ago. So we left the recipe alone and settled for some flavor variations.

Tuna-Spinach Noodle Casserole: Prepare as above, *except* substitute *spinach noodles* for medium noodles, one 10¾-ounce can *condensed cream of celery soup* for mushroom soup, and sliced pitted *ripe olives* for pimiento. Omit Parmesan cheese. Sprinkle with snipped *parsley* before serving.

Tuna-Spaghetti Casserole: Prepare as above, *except* substitute 4 ounces broken *spaghetti* for the noodles and one 10¾-ounce can *condensed tomato soup* for the mushroom soup. Omit peas. Add one 4-ounce can sliced *mushrooms,* drained, and ½ teaspoon dried *oregano,* crushed, with the tuna.

Tuna and Rice Casserole: Prepare as above, *except* substitute 2 cups cooked *rice* for the noodles. Substitute one 11-ounce can *condensed cheddar cheese soup* for the cream of mushroom soup and 1½ cups cooked *broccoli flowerets* for the peas.

Fiesta Tamale Bake

½ **pound bulk pork sausage**
½ **pound ground beef**
1 **medium onion, chopped**
 (½ cup)
½ **cup chopped green pepper**

● In a large skillet cook sausage, ground beef, onion, and green pepper till meat is brown and vegetables are tender. Drain excess fat from skillet.

Adjust the spiciness to suit your taste. For a milder version, use all ground beef and skip the sausage. For added spiciness, use all sausage.

1 **16-ounce can tomatoes,**
 cut up
1 **6-ounce can tomato paste**
¼ **cup sliced pitted ripe**
 olives
1 **tablespoon chili powder**

● Stir in *undrained* tomatoes, tomato paste, olives, and chili powder.

1 **15-ounce can tamales**
½ **cup shredded cheddar**
 cheese (2 ounces)

● Turn meat mixture into a 2-quart casserole. Arrange tamales on top. Bake, uncovered, in a 350° oven for 25 minutes. Sprinkle with cheese. Bake for 5 to 10 minutes more or till heated through. Makes 4 or 5 servings.

Microwave Directions: In a 2-quart microwave-safe casserole crumble sausage and ground beef. Add onion and green pepper. Micro-cook, covered, on 100% power (high) for 5 to 7 minutes or till no pink remains in meat and vegetables are tender, stirring once. Drain excess fat from casserole.

Stir in *undrained* tomatoes, tomato paste, olives, and chili powder. Cook, covered, on high for 2 minutes. Stir. Arrange tamales on top. Cook, uncovered, on high for 6 to 8 minutes or till heated through, giving the dish a half-turn after 3 minutes. Sprinkle with cheese. Cook, uncovered, on high about 30 seconds or till the cheese melts.

Sherry-Sauced Scallops

1 **pound fresh *or* frozen scallops** 4 **ounces fine noodles**	● Thaw scallops, if frozen. Rinse with cold water. Cut any large scallops in half. Drain well. Cook noodles according to package directions. Drain.
1 **small onion, chopped** ¼ **cup chopped celery** 2 **tablespoons margarine *or* butter** 2 **tablespoons all-purpose flour** ¼ **teaspoon salt** ⅛ **teaspoon pepper** **Dash paprika** 1 **cup milk** 1 **2-ounce jar diced pimiento, drained** 2 **tablespoons dry sherry**	● Meanwhile, in a medium saucepan cook onion and celery in margarine or butter till tender. Stir in flour, salt, pepper, and paprika. Add milk all at once. Cook and stir over medium heat till thickened and bubbly. Cook and stir for 1 minute more. Stir in scallops, pimiento, and sherry.
1 **cup plain croutons** 2 **tablespoons margarine *or* butter, melted**	● Arrange noodles in a greased 10x6x2-inch baking dish. Pour scallop mixture over noodles. Toss together croutons and margarine or butter. Sprinkle over casserole. Bake, uncovered, in a 350° oven for 20 to 25 minutes or till scallops are opaque. Makes 4 servings.

Baking scallops in a sherry-flavored sauce on a bed of noodles produces a classy casserole.

Pork and Lentils

2 **slices bacon** 1 **pound boneless pork shoulder, cut into 1-inch cubes**	● In a large skillet cook bacon till crisp. Remove bacon, reserving drippings. Drain bacon on paper towels. Crumble and set aside. Cook pork, *half* at a time, in hot drippings till brown.
¾ **cup dry lentils** 1 **medium onion** 1 **8-ounce can tomato sauce** 1 **7½-ounce can tomatoes, cut up** 1 **tablespoon brown sugar** ¼ **teaspoon salt** ⅛ **teaspoon pepper**	● Rinse lentils with cold water. Cut onion in half lengthwise. Slice each half. In a 1½-quart casserole, stir together tomato sauce, *undrained* tomatoes, brown sugar, salt, pepper, lentils, and onion. Stir in pork and bacon. Bake, covered, in a 350° oven about 1 hour or till pork and lentils are tender, stirring occasionally. Makes 4 servings.

For a new twist on that old favorite, pork and beans, we replaced the beans with lentils.

Chili and Corn Bread Bake

1 **pound ground raw turkey** *or* **ground beef** 1 **medium onion, chopped** **(½ cup)** 1 **clove garlic, minced**	● In a large skillet cook turkey or beef, onion, and garlic till the meat is brown. Drain excess fat from skillet.
1 **8-ounce can tomato sauce** 1 **4-ounce can diced green** **chili peppers, drained** 2 **teaspoons chili powder** ½ **cup shredded Monterey** **Jack cheese (2 ounces)**	● Stir in tomato sauce, chili peppers, and chili powder. Bring to boiling. Remove from heat. Stir in cheese. Turn mixture into a 10x6x2-inch baking dish.
Corn Bread Topping	● Prepare Corn Bread Topping. Spread over meat mixture. Bake in a 350° oven for 20 to 25 minutes or till topping is golden brown. Makes 6 servings.
	Corn Bread Topping: Stir together ½ cup *all-purpose flour,* ½ cup *yellow cornmeal,* 2 tablespoons *sugar,* 2 teaspoons *baking powder, and* ¼ teaspoon *salt.* Add 1 beaten *egg,* ½ cup *milk,* and 2 tablespoons *cooking oil.* Stir just till combined.

Instead of spooning chili over corn bread, cook the two together. In this recipe, the corn bread bakes on top of the chili.

Herbed Chicken and Rice

1 **2½- to 3-pound broiler-** **fryer chicken, quartered** 1 **teaspoon paprika** ½ **teaspoon dried rosemary,** **crushed** ¼ **teaspoon pepper**	● Trim excess fat from chicken quarters. Combine paprika, rosemary, and pepper. Rub on all sides of chicken quarters.
1 **14½-ounce can chicken** **broth** 1 **cup long grain rice** 2 **medium carrots, shredded** **(1 cup)** 1 **4-ounce can mushroom** **stems and pieces,** **drained** ¼ **cup snipped parsley** ¼ **cup dry white wine**	● In a 12x7½x2-inch baking dish combine chicken broth, rice, carrots, mushrooms, parsley, and wine. Arrange chicken quarters on top. Cover dish with foil. Bake in a 350° oven about 1¼ hours or till the chicken and rice are tender. Makes 4 servings.

An herb rub both flavors and colors the chicken quarters.

Chicken Enchiladas

1 **10-ounce can tomatoes with green chili peppers** 1 **teaspoon ground coriander** ¼ **teaspoon ground red pepper (optional)**	● In a blender container combine *undrained* tomatoes, coriander, and, if desired, red pepper. Cover and blend till smooth. Set aside.
1 **medium onion, chopped (½ cup)** 1 **tablespoon cooking oil** 1½ **cups chopped cooked chicken (8 ounces)** 1 **8-ounce carton dairy sour cream** 2 **teaspoons all-purpose flour**	● In a heavy medium skillet cook onion in hot oil till tender. In a mixing bowl combine chicken, *half* of the sour cream, the flour, and cooked onion. Set aside.
8 **6-inch corn tortillas** 2 **tablespoons cooking oil**	● In the same skillet cook tortillas, one at a time, in hot oil about 10 seconds or till limp. Drain on paper towels.
½ **cup shredded Monterey Jack cheese (2 ounces)** **Sliced green onion *and/or* sliced pitted ripe olives (optional)**	● To assemble casserole, spoon about ¼ *cup* of the chicken mixture onto *each* tortilla. Then roll up. Place the filled tortillas, seam side down, in a 10x6x2-inch baking dish. Pour tomato mixture over all. Cover with foil. ⠀⠀Bake in a 350° oven for 15 to 20 minutes or till heated through. Remove foil and top with cheese. Bake for 1 to 2 minutes more or till cheese melts. Top with remaining sour cream, and, if desired green onion and/or sliced ripe olives. Makes 4 servings.

Go for the works. Pile on sour cream, green onions, and olives.

Shortcut Chicken Manicotti

1 **beaten egg**
1 **10-ounce package frozen chopped spinach, thawed and well drained**
1 **cup chopped cooked chicken *or* turkey**
½ **cup cream-style cottage cheese, drained**
¼ **cup grated Parmesan cheese**
10 **manicotti shells**

● For filling, in a mixing bowl combine egg, spinach, chicken or turkey, cottage cheese, and Parmesan cheese. Spoon about ¼ cup of the filling into each *uncooked* manicotti shell. Arrange shells in a 13x9x2-inch baking dish, so they are not touching each other.

1 **10¾-ounce can condensed cream of chicken soup**
1 **8-ounce carton dairy sour cream**
1 **cup milk**
½ **teaspoon Italian seasoning**
1 **cup boiling water**
1 **cup shredded cheddar cheese (4 ounces)**
2 **tablespoons snipped parsley (optional)**

● For sauce, combine soup, sour cream, milk, and Italian seasoning. Pour sauce over manicotti, spreading to cover shells. Slowly pour the boiling water into the dish around the edge. Cover dish tightly with foil. Bake in a 350° oven for 60 to 65 minutes or till the pasta is tender. Sprinkle with cheese and, if desired, parsley. Let stand 10 minutes before serving. Makes 5 servings.

1 To streamline the preparation of this popular pasta casserole, we omitted cooking the manicotti shells in boiling water. Instead, spoon the filling into uncooked shells.

2 Then, arrange the stuffed shells in the baking dish. Leave some space between the shells so they'll cook evenly. Pour sauce over shells. Reposition the shells if they move.

3 Slowly add the boiling water around the edge of the dish. The water is essential for cooking the manicotti shells properly.

Main-Dish Pies

Pies serve as more than desserts. So, we've combined savory fillings with pastry or pasta for delicious, substantial one-dish meals. Spoon into an old-fashioned pot pie or try a wedge of our ever-popular Spaghetti Pie.

Salmon and Artichoke Pie

1 **9-ounce package frozen artichoke hearts, thawed**	● Cut any large artichoke hearts in half. Set aside. In a large saucepan melt margarine or butter. Stir in flour, salt, and pepper till blended. Add milk all at once. Cook and stir over medium heat till mixture is thickened and bubbly. Cook and stir for 1 minute more.
3 **tablespoons margarine _or_ butter**	
3 **tablespoons all-purpose flour**	
¼ **teaspoon salt**	
⅛ **teaspoon pepper**	
1½ **cups milk**	

2 **3-ounce packages cream cheese, cut up**	● Add cream cheese. Stir till melted. Stir in salmon, green onions, dillweed, and artichoke hearts. Turn mixture into an 8x8x2-inch baking dish.
1 **15½-ounce can salmon, drained, flaked, and skin and bones removed**	
2 **green onions, sliced**	
½ **teaspoon dried dillweed**	

½ **of a 17-ounce package (1 sheet) frozen puff pastry sheets, thawed**	● Trim pastry sheet to form an 8-inch square. Cut into six pieces. Arrange pastry pieces over filling. Cut trimmings into shapes with cookie cutters, if desired. Moisten cutouts with water and place on pastry top. Bake in a 375° oven for 30 to 35 minutes or till golden brown. Let stand 10 minutes before serving. Makes 6 servings.

Packaged puff pastry and frozen artichoke hearts dress up this easy, elegant pie. It's perfect for all kinds of special occasions.

Meatball Pie

1	beaten egg
¾	cup soft bread crumbs
¼	cup milk
1	tablespoon dried minced onion
¼	teaspoon salt
¼	teaspoon dried thyme, crushed
¼	teaspoon dried oregano, crushed
⅛	teaspoon pepper
1	pound ground beef

● In a medium mixing bowl combine egg, bread crumbs, milk, onion, salt, thyme, oregano, and pepper. Add ground beef. Mix well. Shape the mixture into 1-inch meatballs.

Arrange meatballs in a shallow baking pan. Bake in a 375° oven for 20 to 25 minutes or till no longer pink. Drain well. Arrange meatballs in an 8x8x2-inch baking dish. Set aside.

Skip a step by using a refrigerated piecrust rather than making your own. Simply trim the pastry to form an 8-inch square. Cut the square into 4 smaller squares. Cut each square diagonally, forming eight triangles. Arrange the triangles over filling and continue as directed in the recipe.

1	medium zucchini, cubed (2 cups)
1	16-ounce can tomatoes, cut up
2	tablespoons tomato paste
2	tablespoons cornstarch
2	teaspoons instant beef bouillon granules
⅛	teaspoon pepper

● In a medium saucepan combine zucchini, *undrained* tomatoes, tomato paste, cornstarch, bouillon granules, and pepper. Cook and stir till thickened and bubbly. Cook and stir for 2 minutes more. Cover and keep warm.

Pot Pie Pastry
Milk

● Roll out pastry into a 9-inch square. Heat zucchini mixture till bubbly. Pour over meatballs. Place pastry over zucchini mixture. Flute edge. Brush pastry with milk.

Bake in a 375° oven for 30 to 35 minutes or till the crust is golden brown. Let stand 10 minutes before serving. Makes 4 servings.

Easy Ground Beef Pie: Omit egg, bread crumbs, and ¼ cup milk. In a large saucepan cook ground beef till brown. Drain fat from pan. Stir in zucchini, *undrained* tomatoes, tomato paste, cornstarch, bouillon granules, onion, salt, thyme, oregano, and ¼ teaspoon pepper. Cook and stir till thickened and bubbly, then cook and stir 2 minutes more. Continue as above.

Pot Pie Pastry

1¼	cups all-purpose flour
⅛	teaspoon salt
⅓	cup shortening
3	to 4 tablespoons cold water

● In a mixing bowl stir together flour and salt. Cut in shortening till pieces are the size of small peas. Sprinkle *1 tablespoon* of the water over part of the mixture; gently toss with a fork. Push to side of bowl. Repeat till all is moistened. Form dough into a ball.

Use this pastry in *Meatball Pie* (above) and *Chicken Pot Pie* (see recipe, page 46).

Spaghetti Pie

Mexicali Macaroni Pie

Greek Pasta Pie

Spaghetti Pie

4 ounces spaghetti
1 beaten egg
⅓ cup grated Parmesan
    cheese
1 tablespoon margarine
    or butter, cut up
	● Cook spaghetti according to package directions. Drain.
	    In a medium mixing bowl combine egg, Parmesan cheese, and margarine or butter. Add spaghetti; toss to coat. Turn into a greased 9-inch pie plate. Press mixture against the bottom and sides of pie plate to form an even crust.

1 beaten egg 1 cup cream-style cottage cheese, drained	● In a small mixing bowl combine egg and cottage cheese. Spread over the spaghetti crust. Set aside.

½ pound ground beef *or* bulk
    Italian sausage
1 medium onion, chopped
    (½ cup)
¼ cup chopped green pepper
¾ cup spaghetti sauce
	● In a large skillet cook ground beef or sausage, onion, and green pepper till the meat is brown. Drain excess fat from skillet. Stir in spaghetti sauce. Cook till heated through.

½ cup shredded mozzarella cheese (2 ounces)	● Spoon meat mixture over cottage cheese layer. Bake, uncovered, in a 350° oven for 20 minutes. Sprinkle with cheese. Bake about 5 minutes more or till cheese is melted. Let stand 5 minutes before serving. Cut into wedges to serve. Makes 4 or 5 servings.

Variety is the spice of life, and that's especially true when it comes to food. That's why each savory pie (pictured opposite) features a different pasta, a different meat filling, and a different cheese.

Mexicali Macaroni Pie: Prepare as directed above, *except* substitute *shell macaroni* for the spaghetti. Omit green pepper and spaghetti sauce. Stir one 8-ounce can *tomato sauce;* one 8-ounce can *red kidney beans,* drained; one 4-ounce can diced *green chili peppers,* drained; and 1 teaspoon *chili powder* into meat mixture. Substitute *Monterey Jack cheese* for the mozzarella cheese. Serve topped with shredded *lettuce* and chopped *tomato.*

Greek Pasta Pie: Prepare as directed above, *except* omit mozzarella cheese and substitute *elbow macaroni* for the spaghetti and *ground lamb* for the ground beef. Stir *half* of one 10-ounce package frozen chopped *spinach,* thawed and drained, into the cottage cheese mixture. Stir ¾ cup *tomato sauce* and ¼ teaspoon ground *cinnamon* into the meat mixture. Before serving, sprinkle with ½ cup crumbled *feta cheese.*

Transatlantic Pie

1 package (8) refrigerated crescent rolls	● Unroll dough and separate into rolls. Arrange in an ungreased 9-inch pie plate, pressing pieces together to form a crust.
1 pound ground beef **1 medium onion, chopped** **1 medium carrot, shredded** **3 tablespoons all-purpose flour** **1 teaspoon dried basil, crushed** **½ teaspoon dried oregano, crushed** **¼ teaspoon fennel seed, crushed** **1 cup milk** **½ cup shredded process Swiss cheese (2 ounces)** **1 cup frozen peas, thawed**	● In a large skillet cook ground beef, onion, and carrot till meat is brown. Drain fat from skillet. Stir in flour, basil, oregano, and fennel seed. Add milk all at once. Cook and stir till thickened and bubbly. Add cheese. Cook and stir till cheese melts. Stir in peas. Turn mixture into unbaked crust.
6 tomato slices **2 tablespoons grated Parmesan cheese**	● Bake in a 350° oven for 20 to 25 minutes or till heated through. Arrange tomato slices over pie. Sprinkle with Parmesan cheese. Bake 2 minutes more. Garnish with parsley, if desired. Let stand 5 minutes before cutting. Serves 6.

Caribbean Beef Pie: Prepare Transatlantic Pie as directed, *except* omit basil, oregano, fennel seed, tomato, and Parmesan cheese. Add 2 tablespoons chopped canned *green chili peppers,* 1 teaspoon finely shredded *lime peel,* and ¼ teaspoon *ground red pepper* with the flour. Bake in a 350° oven for 20 to 25 minutes. Arrange 6 thin slices *Edam cheese* on top. Bake for 1 minute more. Garnish with sliced red and green *chili peppers,* if desired.

Middle Eastern Beef Pie: Prepare Transatlantic Pie as directed, *except* omit basil, oregano, fennel seed, tomato, and Parmesan cheese. Add ½ teaspoon dried *mint,* crushed, with the flour. Bake in a 350° oven for 20 to 25 minutes. Dollop ½ cup plain *yogurt* or *dairy sour cream* over top of pie. Garnish with halved *cucumber slices,* if desired.

Upside-Down Pizza

1 pound ground turkey sausage *or* bulk Italian sausage
1 medium onion, chopped (½ cup)
½ cup chopped green pepper

● In a medium skillet cook sausage, onion, and green pepper till meat is brown and vegetables are tender. Drain fat from skillet.

The crust is on top and the toppings are on the bottom of this pizzalike casserole.

1 15-ounce can pizza sauce
¼ cup sliced pitted ripe olives
1 2-ounce can mushroom stems and pieces, drained
2 ounces sliced pepperoni (optional)
¼ teaspoon crushed red pepper
1 cup shredded mozzarella cheese (4 ounces)
1 10-ounce package refrigerated pizza dough
¼ cup grated Parmesan cheese

● Stir in pizza sauce, olives, mushrooms, pepperoni (if desired), and crushed red pepper. Cook till heated through. Turn mixture into a 10x6x2-inch baking dish. Sprinkle with mozzarella cheese.

Unroll pizza dough. Cut into 5 lengthwise strips. Gently roll each strip into a 10-inch rope. Lay 3 ropes lengthwise atop meat mixture. Cut remaining strips in half crosswise forming 4 pieces. Weave these strips atop to make a lattice crust. Sprinkle with Parmesan cheese. Bake in a 400° oven for about 20 minutes or till the crust is golden brown. Makes 4 servings.

Tourtière

1½ pounds ground pork	● In a large skillet cook the pork till brown. Drain fat from skillet.	**French Canadians traditionally serve this pork and potato pie on Christmas Eve.**

1½ pounds ground pork
2 large potatoes, peeled and chopped (2¼ cups)
1 medium onion, finely chopped (½ cup)
½ cup beef broth
1 clove garlic, minced
1 bay leaf
½ teaspoon salt
¼ teaspoon ground ginger
⅛ teaspoon pepper
Dash ground cloves

● In a large skillet cook the pork till brown. Drain fat from skillet.

In a medium saucepan combine potatoes, onion, beef broth, garlic, and bay leaf. Bring to boiling. Reduce heat. Cover and simmer about 10 minutes or till potatoes are tender. *Do not drain.* Remove bay leaf. Mash potato mixture. Stir in pork, salt, ginger, pepper, and cloves. Set aside.

French Canadians traditionally serve this pork and potato pie on Christmas Eve.

Tourtière Pastry (recipe below)

● Prepare pastry. On a lightly floured surface, roll out *half* of the pastry to form a 12-inch circle. Line a 9-inch pie plate with pastry. Trim to ½ inch beyond edge. Fill pastry shell with meat mixture. Roll out remaining pastry to form another 12-inch circle. Place over filling. Seal and flute edge (see photo, top right). Cut slits in top crust (see photo, bottom right). Bake in a 400° oven for 25 to 30 minutes or till golden brown. Makes 6 servings.

To flute the edge, place your thumb against the inside edge of the pie shell. Press the dough around your thumb using the index finger and thumb of your other hand.

Tourtière Pastry: In a medium mixing bowl stir together 2 cups *all-purpose flour,* 2 teaspoons *baking powder,* ½ teaspoon dried *thyme* (crushed), and ¼ teaspoon *salt.* Cut in ⅔ cup *shortening* till pieces are the size of small peas. Set aside.

Stir together 1 beaten *egg,* ¼ cup *cold water,* and 1 teaspoon *lemon juice.* Sprinkle egg mixture over flour mixture, 1 tablespoon at a time, tossing gently with a fork. Divide mixture in half. Shape each half into a ball.

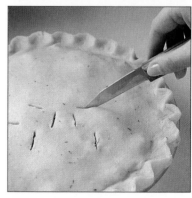

Use a sharp knife to cut slits in the pie top. The slits allow the steam that forms during baking to escape.

Chicken Pot Pies

Pot Pie Pastry (see recipe, page 39)

● Prepare pastry. Divide into 3 balls and flatten slightly. On a lightly floured surface roll each ball into a circle ½ inch larger than a 15-ounce casserole. Cut pastry trimmings into decorative shapes with cookie cutters, if desired. Cover rounds and cutouts and set aside.

If you don't have three 15-ounce casseroles, one 2-quart casserole or six 10-ounce individual casseroles work just as well. Roll out the pastry to ⅛-inch thickness. Cut the pastry ½ inch larger than the diameter of the casserole top. For the 2-quart casserole, increase baking time to 25 to 30 minutes.

1 medium onion, chopped (½ cup)
¼ cup margarine *or* butter
½ cup all-purpose flour
1 tablespoon instant chicken bouillon granules
½ teaspoon poultry seasoning
⅛ teaspoon pepper
2 cups milk

● In a large saucepan cook onion in margarine or butter till tender but not brown. Stir in flour, bouillon granules, poultry seasoning, and pepper. Add milk all at once. Cook and stir till thickened and bubbly.

3 cups chopped cooked chicken *or* turkey
1 10-ounce package frozen peas and carrots
1 4-ounce can sliced mushrooms, drained
¼ cup snipped parsley
1 beaten egg
1 teaspoon water

● Stir in chicken, peas and carrots, mushrooms, and parsley. Cook till bubbly. Season with salt and pepper.

Turn hot filling into three 15-ounce casseroles. Place pastry circles over individual casseroles. Flute edges. Top with pastry cutouts. Cut slits in top to let steam escape.

Combine egg and water. Brush over pastry. Place pot pies on baking sheet in oven. Bake in a 450° oven for 15 to 20 minutes or till the crust is golden brown. Makes 6 servings.

Beef Pot Pie: Prepare as above, *except* substitute crushed dried *thyme* for the poultry seasoning, instant *beef bouillon granules* for the chicken bouillon granules, chopped cooked *beef* for the chicken, and frozen *mixed vegetables* for the peas and carrots.

Pork Pot Pie: Prepare as above, *except* substitute crushed dried *marjoram* for the poultry seasoning, chopped cooked *pork* for the chicken, and frozen *corn* for the peas and carrots.

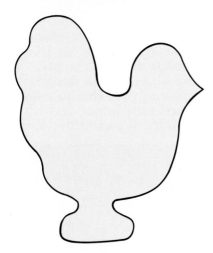

Make-Ahead Casseroles

Time spent cooking one day means carefree cooking on another.
Set aside an afternoon to mix up a casserole or two. Then,
stash them in your freezer. When you're ready to eat one, pop it
in the oven and relax till chow time. You can
bake these recipes without freezing, too. Just reduce the baking
time, cooking only till hot and bubbly.

Curried Chicken Pilaf

2 whole large chicken breasts (about 2 pounds total), skinned, boned, and halved lengthwise 2 tablespoons cooking oil	● Cut chicken into bite-size pieces. In a large skillet cook chicken, *half* at a time, in hot oil about 4 minutes or till no longer pink, stirring frequently. Remove chicken, reserving drippings.
1 cup sliced fresh mushrooms 1 cup chopped sweet red *or* green pepper 1 medium onion, chopped (½ cup) 1 14½-ounce can chicken broth ⅔ cup converted long grain rice 1 to 2 teaspoons curry powder ⅛ teaspoon garlic powder	● Cook mushrooms, pepper, and onion in drippings (add more oil, if necessary) about 5 minutes or till tender. Stir in chicken broth, rice, curry powder, and garlic powder. Bring to boiling. Reduce heat. Cover and simmer about 20 minutes or till rice is tender.
1 8-ounce can sliced water chestnuts, drained ½ cup peanuts ½ cup raisins	● Stir in chicken, water chestnuts, peanuts, and raisins. Turn mixture into a 12x7½x2-inch baking dish. Cool slightly. Wrap in foil, label, and freeze.
	● To serve, bake frozen casserole, covered, in a 375° oven about 1¼ hours or till heated through. Makes 5 servings.

Curry powder blends many spices into one. Although the ingredients vary by manufacturer, most combine allspice, cardamom, cinnamon, cloves, fennel, ginger, mace, mustard, and pepper.

Ham and Broccoli Bake

⅔ cup converted long grain rice 1 10-ounce package frozen cut broccoli	● Cook rice according to package directions, *except* omit salt. Set aside. Run water over broccoli to separate.
3 tablespoons margarine *or* butter 1 medium onion, chopped (½ cup) ¼ cup all-purpose flour ⅛ teaspoon pepper 2½ cups milk 2 cups cubed fully cooked ham	● In a medium saucepan melt the margarine or butter. Add onion and cook till tender. Stir in flour and pepper. Add milk all at once. Cook and stir till mixture is thickened and bubbly. Cook and stir for 1 minute more. Stir in ham. Remove from heat. In a 12x7½x2-inch baking dish layer the ham mixture, rice, and broccoli. Cool slightly. Wrap with foil, label, and freeze.
6 slices American cheese ¾ cup soft bread crumbs (1 slice) 1 tablespoon margarine *or* butter, melted	● To serve, bake frozen casserole, covered, in a 375° oven for 1 hour. Remove cover. Arrange cheese slices on top. Combine bread crumbs and margarine or butter. Sprinkle over cheese. Bake for 10 to 15 minutes more or till heated through. Makes 6 servings.

Be sure to use converted rice in casseroles destined for the freezer. It retains a firm texture even after freezing.

Meatball and Bean Stew

1 beaten egg ¼ cup fine dry bread crumbs ¼ cup milk ½ teaspoon Italian seasoning ¼ teaspoon garlic powder 1 pound ground beef	● Combine egg, bread crumbs, milk, Italian seasoning, garlic powder, ¼ teaspoon *salt*, and ⅛ teaspoon *pepper*. Add beef. Mix well. Shape into 1-inch meatballs.
1 tablespoon cooking oil 2 medium carrots, thinly sliced 1 medium onion, chopped (½ cup) ½ cup chopped green pepper 1 15½-ounce jar meatless spaghetti sauce 1 15-ounce can great northern beans	● In a 12-inch skillet cook the meatballs in hot oil till brown, turning occasionally. Remove meatballs. Add carrots, onion, and green pepper. Cook and stir till tender. Drain fat. Add spaghetti sauce and *undrained* beans. Gently stir in meatballs. Turn mixture into a 2-quart casserole. Cool slightly. Wrap with foil, label, and freeze.
Grated Parmesan cheese	● To serve, bake frozen casserole, covered, in a 375° oven about 1½ hours or till heated through, stirring gently once. Serve with Parmesan cheese. Makes 4 servings.

If you want your stew *now,* not later, heat the mixture in the skillet till it's hot and bubbly.

Southern-Style Casserole

½ cup converted long grain rice
4 slices bacon
1 large onion, chopped
1 stalk celery, chopped
½ cup chopped green pepper

● Cook rice according to package directions. Set aside.
    In a skillet cook bacon till crisp. Remove bacon, reserving 2 tablespoons drippings. Drain, crumble, and set aside.
    Cook onion, celery, and green pepper in drippings till tender. Set aside.

This flavorful recipe starts with a Southern favorite, black-eyed peas. Cooks below the Mason-Dixon Line serve dishes like this on New Year's Day to bring good luck all year.

2 cups chopped cooked pork
2 15-ounce cans black-eyed peas, drained
1 8-ounce can tomato sauce
1 7½-ounce can tomatoes, cut up
1 tablespoon Worcestershire sauce
¼ teaspoon bottled hot pepper sauce

● In a large mixing bowl combine pork, black-eyed peas, tomato sauce, *undrained* tomatoes, Worcestershire sauce, hot pepper sauce, pepper, rice, bacon, ⅛ teaspoon *pepper*, and onion mixture. Turn into a 2-quart casserole. Cover with plastic wrap. Wrap with foil, label, and freeze.

● To serve, remove plastic wrap. Bake frozen casserole, covered, in a 350° oven for 1¼ to 1½ hours or till heated through, stirring once. Makes 6 servings.

Brunswick Bake

2 10-ounce packages frozen succotash
2 to 2½ pounds meaty chicken pieces (breasts, thighs, and drumsticks)
2 tablespoons cooking oil

● Run water over frozen succotash to separate. Remove skin from chicken, if desired. In a 12-inch skillet brown chicken in hot oil. Transfer chicken to a 13x9x2-inch baking dish. Reserve 2 tablespoons of the drippings.

The tomato mixture will seem exceptionally thick when you make it, but it thins to just the right consistency after you freeze and bake the casserole.

1 large onion, chopped
2 tablespoons all-purpose flour
1 0.7-ounce envelope Italian salad dressing mix
1 8-ounce can stewed tomatoes, cut up
1 bay leaf

● Cook onion in reserved drippings till tender. Stir in flour and salad dressing mix. Add *undrained* tomatoes and bay leaf. Cook and stir till thickened and bubbly. Cook and stir for 1 minute more. Stir in succotash. Pour over chicken. Cool slightly. Cover with plastic wrap. Wrap with foil, label, and freeze.

● To serve, remove plastic wrap. Bake frozen casserole, covered, in a 375° oven for 1 to 1¼ hours or till chicken is tender. To serve, remove chicken pieces. Stir the vegetable mixture, then serve with chicken. Makes 4 servings.

Sausage Twist Casserole

1 **cup corkscrew macaroni** 1 **pound bulk pork *or* ground turkey sausage** ½ **cup sliced celery** ¼ **cup chopped onion**	● Cook macaroni in boiling salted water for 5 to 6 minutes or till almost tender. Rinse in cold water. Drain and set aside. Meanwhile, in a large skillet cook sausage, celery, and onion till sausage is brown and vegetables are tender. Drain excess fat from skillet.	**Cook the macaroni just till it's almost tender. Then, place it in a colander and rinse with cold water to halt any further cooking. The macaroni will finish cooking when you bake the frozen casserole.**
2 **cups loose-pack frozen mixed vegetables** 1 **14½-ounce can tomatoes, cut up** 1 **6-ounce can tomato paste** ¼ **cup grated Parmesan cheese** ½ **teaspoon dried oregano, crushed** ¼ **teaspoon garlic powder** ¼ **teaspoon dried basil, crushed**	● Stir frozen vegetables, *undrained* tomatoes, tomato paste, cheese, oregano, garlic powder, basil, and macaroni into the skillet. Stir till well combined. Spoon mixture into an 8x8x2-inch baking dish. Cool slightly. Cover with plastic wrap. Wrap in foil, label, and freeze.	
Grated Parmesan cheese (optional)	● To serve, bake frozen casserole, covered, in a 375° oven about 1¼ hours or till heated through, stirring occasionally. Sprinkle with additional Parmesan cheese, if desired. Serves 4.	

Some Freezer Tips

To make the most efficient use of your freezer, keep these points in mind:
● Set your freezer temperature at 0° F or below to maintain the best food color, flavor, and texture. A freezer thermometer will help you check on the temperature in your freezer.
● When you add a casserole to the freezer, separate it from the other packages until it's solidly frozen. This allows the cold air to circulate around the casserole.
● Let foods freeze as quickly as possible by limiting how much food you add to the freezer at one time. Freeze only two to three pounds of food per cubic foot of total storage space within a 24-hour period.
● Freeze casseroles up to three months. Label and date each casserole when you freeze it. Then you can quickly identify the package and know when to use it.

Chicken Lasagna Rosettes

Lasagna noodles form the rosettes in this elegant chicken and mushroom casserole.

4 **whole medium chicken breasts (about 3 pounds total), skinned, boned, and halved lengthwise** 8 **ounces fresh mushrooms, sliced** 1 **medium onion, finely chopped (½ cup)** ¼ **cup margarine *or* butter** ¾ **cup dry white wine** ½ **teaspoon salt** ½ **teaspoon white pepper** ¼ **teaspoon dried tarragon, crushed**	● Cut chicken into 1-inch pieces. For filling, in a large skillet cook mushrooms and onion in margarine or butter till tender. Stir in chicken, wine, salt, white pepper, and tarragon. Bring to boiling. Reduce heat. Cover and simmer for 8 to 10 minutes or till the chicken is tender.
8 **lasagna noodles**	● Cook lasagna noodles according to package directions. Drain. Cut each noodle in half lengthwise. Curl each into a 2½-inch diameter ring. Arrange rings in a 13x9x2-inch baking dish. Using a slotted spoon, spoon filling into lasagna rings, reserving the broth in skillet.
½ **cup light cream *or* milk** ½ **cup dairy sour cream** 4 **teaspoons cornstarch** 1 **8-ounce package cream cheese, cut up** 1½ **cups shredded Gruyère cheese (6 ounces)** 1 **cup shredded Muenster cheese (4 ounces)**	● For sauce, in a small bowl combine cream or milk, sour cream, and cornstarch. Add to broth in skillet. Cook and stir till thickened and bubbly. Add cream cheese, *half* of the Gruyère cheese, and *half* of the Muenster cheese. Cook and stir till cheese is melted. Spoon over lasagna rings. Sprinkle remaining cheese over rings. Cool slightly. Wrap with foil, label, and freeze.
3 **tablespoons slivered almonds, toasted (optional)** 3 **tablespoons snipped parsley (optional)**	● To serve, thaw casserole overnight in the refrigerator. Bake, covered, in a 375° oven for 1¼ to 1½ hours or till heated through. Let stand for 10 minutes before serving. Sprinkle with the almonds and parsley, if desired. Makes 8 servings.

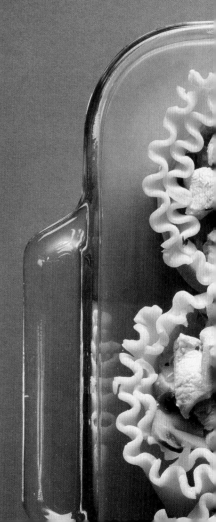

1 Cut the cooked lasagna noodles lengthwise in half. Curl each half into a ring about 2½ inches in diameter. Arrange the noodle rings in the baking dish.

2 Add the chicken filling to the center of the lasagna rings. Then spoon the sauce over the pasta and filling, and sprinkle with cheese. Now it's ready to freeze.

Eggplant Pasta Casserole

4 ounces elbow *or* corkscrew macaroni	● Cook macaroni according to package directions. Drain.	A trio of cheeses—ricotta, mozzarella, and Parmesan—team up with the pasta to provide the protein in this meatless main dish.
1 small eggplant (about 12 ounces), peeled and cut into ½-inch cubes 1 medium onion, chopped 2 cloves garlic, minced 2 tablespoons cooking oil 1 16-ounce can tomatoes, cut up 1 6-ounce can tomato paste ½ teaspoon dried oregano, crushed ½ teaspoon dried basil, crushed	● In a large saucepan cook eggplant, onion, and garlic in hot oil till tender. Stir in *undrained* tomatoes, tomato paste, oregano, basil, and ¼ teaspoon *salt.* Bring to boiling. Reduce heat. Simmer, uncovered, for 10 minutes. Remove from heat. Stir in macaroni.	
1 15-ounce carton ricotta cheese 1 cup shredded mozzarella cheese (4 ounces) ½ cup grated Parmesan cheese 2 tablespoons snipped parsley	● Turn *half* of the eggplant mixture into a 12x7½x2-inch baking dish. Combine ricotta cheese, mozzarella cheese, *half* of the Parmesan cheese, and the parsley. Spread over eggplant mixture. Top with the remaining eggplant mixture. Sprinkle with the remaining Parmesan cheese. Cool slightly. Cover with plastic wrap. Wrap with foil, label, and freeze.	
	● To serve, remove plastic wrap. Bake frozen casserole, covered, in a 350° oven for 1¼ hours. Bake, uncovered, for 15 to 20 minutes more or till heated through. Makes 6 servings.	

Versatile Freezer Wraps

To keep your baking dishes and casseroles free for cooking, wrap your make-ahead recipes this way: Cut a length of heavy-duty foil three times the width or diameter of the dish. Line the casserole or dish with the foil. Add the food and cool. Bring the longer sides of the foil together over the food. Fold down the foil, pressing the air out, until the foil is next to the food. Fold down the shorter sides of the foil. Freeze until firm. Then lift the foil-wrapped food from the dish. Label and store in the freezer. When you're ready to reheat, remove the foil and return the frozen food to the original dish. You'll get an exact fit every time.

Make-Ahead Lasagna Rolls

8	lasagna noodles	
¾	pound ground beef	
1	medium onion, chopped	
1	clove garlic, minced	
1	cup ricotta cheese	
1	cup shredded mozzarella cheese (4 ounces)	
¼	cup grated Parmesan cheese	
¼	cup snipped parsley	

● Cook lasagna noodles according to package directions. Drain. Rinse with cold water. Drain again and set aside.

For filling, in a large skillet cook ground beef, onion, and garlic till meat is brown. Drain off excess fat. Stir in ricotta cheese, mozzarella cheese, Parmesan cheese, and parsley.

2 cups chunky spaghetti sauce

● Spread about ⅓ cup filling over each lasagna noodle. Roll up. Place, seam side down, in a 12x7½x2-inch baking dish. Spoon spaghetti sauce over rolls. Cover with plastic wrap. Wrap with foil, label, and freeze.

½ cup shredded mozzarella cheese (2 ounces)

● To serve, remove plastic wrap. Bake frozen lasagna rolls, covered, in a 375° oven for 1 to 1¼ hours or till heated through. Sprinkle with cheese. Bake for 1 to 2 minutes more or till cheese melts. Makes 4 servings.

To serve *Make-Ahead Lasagna Rolls* tonight instead of next week, skip the freezing step and bake them in a 375° oven about 35 minutes.

Basil Turkey With Rice

½	cup converted long grain rice	
1¾	cups milk	
3	tablespoons cornstarch	
¾	teaspoon dried basil, crushed	
1	cup shredded process Swiss cheese (4 ounces)	
¼	cup dry white wine	

● Cook rice according to package directions.

Meanwhile, for sauce, in a medium saucepan stir together milk and cornstarch. Add basil, ½ teaspoon *salt*, and ⅛ teaspoon *pepper*. Cook and stir till thickened and bubbly. Add cheese. Cook and stir till cheese melts. Remove saucepan from heat. Stir in wine. Measure ⅔ cup sauce; set aside.

1	10-ounce package frozen cut asparagus, thawed
1	2½-ounce jar sliced mushrooms, drained
4	turkey breast tenderloin steaks (about 1 pound)

● Stir asparagus, mushrooms, and cooked rice into the remaining sauce in saucepan. Spread in a 12x7½x2-inch baking dish. Arrange turkey steaks on top. Spread reserved sauce over turkey steaks. Wrap with foil, label, and freeze.

Paprika

● To serve, bake, covered, in 375° oven 1¾ to 2 hours or till turkey is tender. Sprinkle with paprika. Makes 4 servings.

Let's talk turkey. Turkey tenderloin steaks are ½-inch-thick lengthwise slices from the breast.

The dish and the wrap play important roles in the success of your frozen dinner. Use baking dishes or casseroles that are recommended for freezer to oven or freezer to microwave oven. Overwrap casseroles with heavy-duty foil to keep air and moisture out. Wrap the foil tightly around the food and the dish. If the recipe includes an acidic ingredient, such as a tomato product, wrap the food first in clear plastic wrap. Then overwrap with foil. Remember to remove the plastic wrap before you bake the casserole.

Spanish Seafood With Rice

8 ounces bulk Italian sausage **1 medium onion, chopped (½ cup)** **½ cup chopped celery** **½ cup chopped green pepper** **1 clove garlic, minced**	● In a 12-inch skillet cook sausage, onion, celery, green pepper, and garlic till sausage is brown and vegetables are tender. Drain fat from skillet.
1 16-ounce can tomatoes, cut up **1 10-ounce can whole baby clams** **1 cup converted long grain rice** **1 cup chicken broth** **⅛ teaspoon ground saffron** **1 10-ounce package frozen peas**	● Stir in *undrained* tomatoes, *undrained* clams, rice, chicken broth, and ground saffron. Bring to boiling. Reduce heat. Cover and simmer for 10 minutes. Stir in peas. Turn sausage mixture into a 3-quart casserole. Cover with plastic wrap. Cool slightly. Wrap with foil, label, and freeze.
1 pound fresh *or* frozen shrimp in shells	● To serve, remove plastic wrap. Bake frozen casserole in a 375° oven, covered, for 1½ hours. Meanwhile, peel shrimp under running water. Remove vein that runs down back. Stir sausage mixture. Then, stir in shrimp. Bake about 30 minutes more or till rice is tender and shrimp turn pink. Stir again before serving. Makes 8 servings.

Shrimp, clams, sausage, and rice costar in this hearty dish reminiscent of Spanish paella.

Potluck Casseroles

Casseroles taste even better in the company of friends, and the more, the merrier. No wonder potlucks are as popular now as ever. You'll find recipes on the following pages that serve a crowd. Each one makes enough to serve you, your family, and more.

Garden Beef And Rice Bake

1 cup long grain rice
2 pounds ground beef
2 stalks celery, sliced (1 cup)
1 large onion, chopped
   (1 cup)

● Cook rice according to package directions. Set aside.
   Meanwhile, in a 12-inch skillet cook ground beef, celery, and onion till beef is brown and vegetables are tender. Drain off fat.

Nacho cheese soup gives a little kick to this tasty dish. If you have trouble locating the nacho variety, try a plain cheese soup mix instead.

1 medium zucchini
   (8 ounces)
2 medium tomatoes,
   chopped
2 cups milk
1 4-ounce can sliced
   mushrooms, drained
1 3-ounce package
   (2 envelopes) nacho
   cheese soup mix
2 teaspoons dried basil,
   crushed
¼ teaspoon pepper
1 cup shredded cheddar
   cheese (4 ounces)

● Trim the ends from zucchini. Cut zucchini in half lengthwise, then slice each half crosswise.
   In a 13x9x2-inch baking dish combine meat mixture, rice, zucchini, tomatoes, milk, mushrooms, soup mix, basil, and pepper. Mix well.
   Bake, covered, in a 375° oven for 30 to 35 minutes or till heated through. Stir before serving. Sprinkle with cheese. Makes 8 servings.

Beef and Bean Stew

⅓ cup all-purpose flour 1 envelope *regular* onion soup mix 3 to 4 teaspoons chili powder ¼ teaspoon pepper 1½ pounds beef stew meat, cut into 1-inch cubes	● In a plastic bag combine flour, soup mix, chili powder, and pepper. Add beef cubes. Shake to coat. Place beef cubes in a 3-quart casserole.
1 12-ounce can beer 1 large green pepper, chopped (1 cup) ⅔ cup water	● Gradually stir in beer, green pepper, and water. Bake, covered, in a 350° oven for 1½ hours.
1 16-ounce can golden hominy, drained 1 15-ounce can great northern beans, drained 1 15-ounce can red kidney beans, drained Shredded American *or* cheddar cheese (optional)	● Stir in hominy and beans. Bake, covered, for 20 to 30 minutes more or till the beef is tender. Sprinkle with cheese, if desired. Makes 8 servings.

Take along a loaf of French bread to serve with this hearty stew. Slice, butter, and wrap the bread in foil. Then, heat in the oven with the stew for the last 5 to 10 minutes of the baking time.

Three-Bean And Ham Bake

2 16-ounce cans pork and beans with tomato sauce 1 15-ounce can butter beans, drained 1 15-ounce can red kidney beans, drained ½ cup catsup 1 tablespoon dried minced onion 1 tablespoon prepared mustard 1½ pounds fully cooked ham, cut into cubes (4½ cups)	● In a 3-quart casserole combine pork and beans, butter beans, kidney beans, catsup, minced onion, and mustard. Mix well. Stir in ham. Bake, covered, in a 350° oven about 30 minutes or till heated through. Makes 8 servings.

For a family-size recipe (to serve 4), use 8-ounce cans of butter and kidney beans and cut the remaining ingredients in half. Bake in a 1½-quart casserole about 30 minutes.

Ham, Turkey, And Noodles

6 **ounces medium noodles**	● Cook noodles according to package directions. Drain.

Feed an army of hungry folks with this crunchy-topped casserole.

2 **8-ounce cartons dairy sour cream** 1 **12-ounce jar chicken** *or* **turkey gravy** ¾ **teaspoon dried thyme, crushed** ¼ **teaspoon pepper** 2 **cups fully cooked ham cut into bite-size strips** 2 **cups chopped cooked turkey** *or* **chicken** 1 **16-ounce package frozen peas and carrots** 1 **4-ounce can sliced mushrooms, drained**	● In a large mixing bowl combine sour cream, gravy, thyme, and pepper. Stir in ham, turkey or chicken, peas and carrots, mushrooms, and noodles. Turn into a 13x9x2-inch baking dish.
½ **cup crushed rich round crackers** ⅓ **cup chopped pecans** *or* **walnuts** 2 **tablespoons margarine** *or* **butter, melted**	● Bake, covered, in a 375° oven for 45 minutes, stirring once. Combine crushed crackers and nuts. Toss with margarine or butter. Sprinkle over casserole. Bake, uncovered, for 5 to 10 minutes more or till heated through. Serves 8 to 10.

Serve It Hot!

To keep your casserole hot until you reach your potluck supper, wrap it in foil or a heavy towel and place it in a plastic-foam container. Some inexpensive square or round foam containers often are sized just right for a 1- or 2-quart casserole. Remember, pack up the casserole as soon as you take it from the oven.

exas-Style Casserole

In a 12-inch skillet cook meat and ion till meat is brown. Drain excess fat m skillet. Stir in kidney beans, tomato uce, chili peppers, chili powder, garlic wder, and pepper. Cook till heated rough. Remove from heat.

We used popular Tex-Mex ingredients to create a chili and corn bread sandwich that you bake in a dish.

In a medium mixing bowl stir together ½ cups cornmeal, baking soda, and alt. Stir in milk, eggs, and *undrained* orn. Stir in cheese and chili peppers. Mix till well blended.

Sprinkle a thin layer of cornmeal over the bottom of a greased 13x9x2-inch baking dish. Spread *half* of the batter evenly in dish. Spoon meat mixture over the batter in dish. Top with the remaining batter.

Bake in a 350° oven for 45 to 50 minutes or till golden brown. Let stand 15 minutes. Serve with salsa and sour cream, if desired. Makes 8 servings.

cheese (

1 4-ounce can diced green chili peppers, drained
Yellow cornmeal
Salsa (optional)
Dairy sour cream (optional)

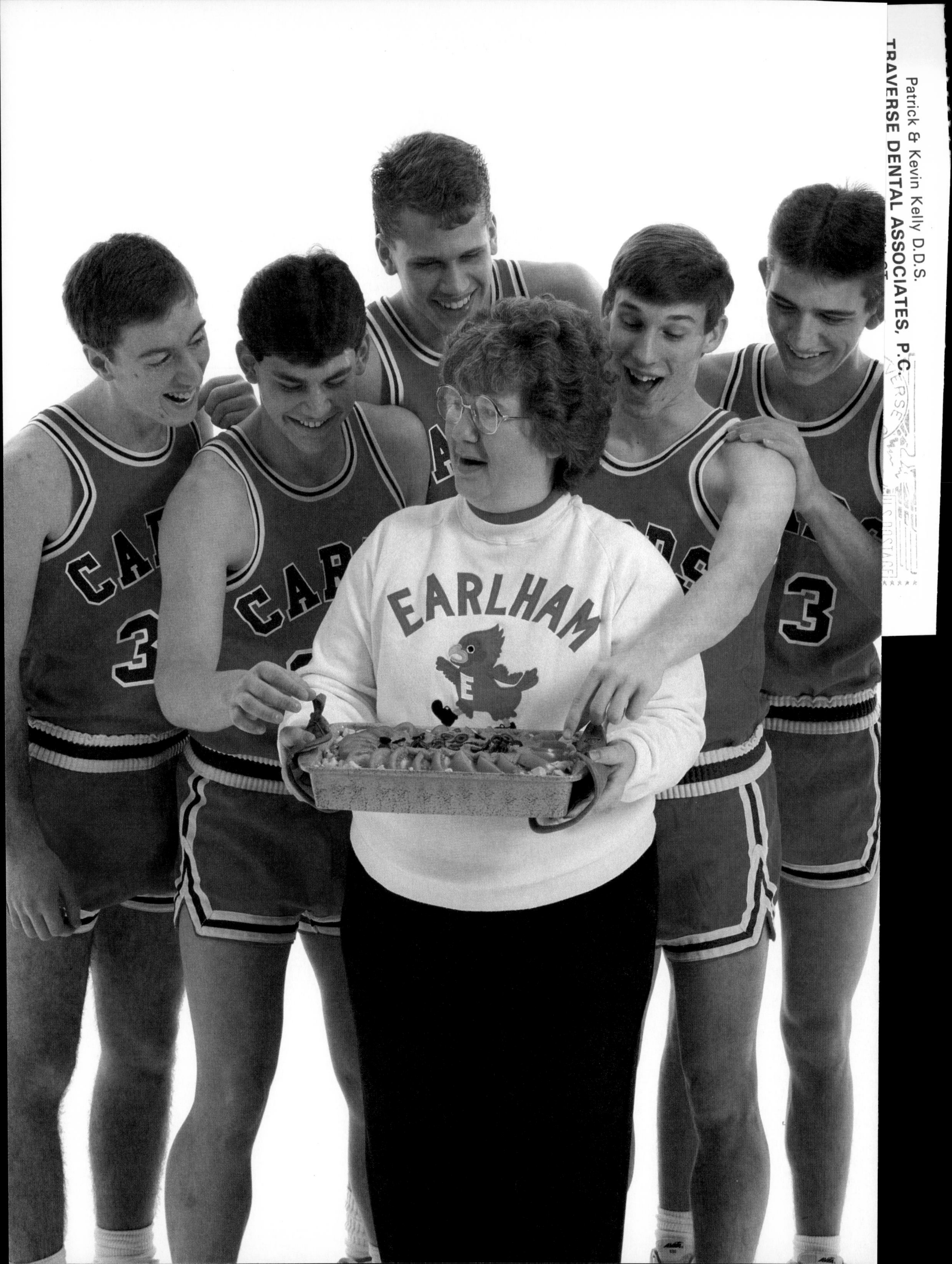
EARLHAM
Patrick & Kevin Kelly D.D.S.
TRAVERSE DENTAL ASSOCIATES, P.C.

Zippy Chicken Casserole

2 cups whole wheat *or* plain elbow macaroni 1 10-ounce package frozen chopped broccoli	● Cook macaroni according to package directions. Drain. Meanwhile, run water over broccoli to thaw.
¼ cup margarine *or* butter 1 large onion, chopped ½ cup thinly sliced celery ¼ cup all-purpose flour Several dashes bottled hot pepper sauce Dash pepper 2 cups milk 1½ cups shredded American cheese (6 ounces)	● For sauce, in a large saucepan melt margarine or butter. Add onion and celery. Cook till tender. Stir in flour, pepper sauce, and pepper. Add milk all at once. Cook and stir over medium heat till mixture is thickened and bubbly. Add cheese. Cook and stir till cheese melts.
3 cups chopped cooked chicken *or* turkey ½ cup sliced pitted ripe olives 2 medium tomatoes, sliced 1 6-ounce container frozen Mexican-style avocado dip, thawed ½ cup alfalfa sprouts (optional)	● Add chicken or turkey, olives, macaroni, and broccoli to sauce. Mix well. Turn mixture into a 13x9x2-inch baking dish. Bake, covered, in a 350° oven for 30 minutes. Arrange tomato slices over top. Bake, covered, about 5 minutes more or till heated through. Spoon avocado dip over top. Sprinkle with alfalfa sprouts, if desired. Serves 8.

This avocado-topped chicken casserole normally feeds eight, but if you're feeding a hungry basketball team, count on fewer servings.

Chicken Stuffing Bake

½ cup long grain rice
1 medium onion, chopped (½ cup)
½ cup chopped green pepper
1 tablespoon margarine *or* butter

● Cook rice according to package directions. Meanwhile, in a small skillet cook onion and green pepper in margarine or butter till tender. Remove from heat and set aside.

To keep the sauce warm until you arrive at the potluck, pack it in a wide-mouthed insulated vacuum bottle.

1 8-ounce package herb-seasoned stuffing mix
2 cups water
4 cups finely chopped cooked chicken *or* turkey
3 beaten eggs
1 10¾-ounce can condensed cream of chicken soup
1 2-ounce jar diced pimiento, drained

● In a large mixing bowl combine stuffing mix and water. Stir in chicken or turkey, eggs, *half* of the soup, the pimiento, cooked rice, and onion mixture. Mix well. Spread mixture in a greased 13x9x2-inch baking dish.

Bake, uncovered, in a 350° oven for 25 to 30 minutes or till heated through. Let stand 5 minutes before serving.

½ cup dairy sour cream
¼ cup milk

● Meanwhile, for sauce, in a small saucepan combine remaining soup, the sour cream, and milk. Cook over low heat till heated through. Cut casserole into squares to serve. Spoon sauce over each serving. Makes 8 servings.

Fast-Cooking Chicken

Many casseroles start with cooked poultry, and one of the shortest paths to cooked chicken is through the door of your microwave oven. Here's how: Place boneless, skinless chicken breast halves in a 10x6x2-inch baking dish. Cover with vented microwave-safe plastic wrap. Micro-cook on 100% power (high) for 1½ minutes for 8 ounces of chicken, 3 minutes for 1 pound.

Rearrange and turn chicken pieces over (move outside pieces to the center of the dish). Then cook, covered, on high for ½ to 1½ minutes more for 8 ounces, 3 to 4 minutes more for 1 pound, or till no longer pink. One pound of boneless chicken breasts yields about 2½ cups chopped cooked chicken.

Sweet and Sour Drumsticks

1 cup long grain rice 16 chicken drumsticks *or* thighs (3½ to 4 pounds total) 2 tablespoons cooking oil	● Cook the rice according to package directions. Set aside. Meanwhile, in a large skillet cook *half* of the chicken drumsticks or thighs in hot oil till brown on all sides. Remove chicken from skillet and set aside. Repeat with remaining chicken.
1 large green *or* sweet red pepper, chopped 1 medium onion, chopped (½ cup) 1 clove garlic, minced	● Add green or sweet red pepper, onion, and garlic to drippings in skillet. Cook till tender. Set aside.
2 16-ounce cans fancy mixed Chinese vegetables, drained 1 15-ounce can tomato sauce ¼ cup packed brown sugar ¼ cup wine vinegar 2 tablespoons soy sauce ¼ teaspoon ground ginger	● In a 13x9x2-inch baking dish combine Chinese vegetables, rice, and cooked pepper mixture. Arrange chicken on top. Season chicken with salt and pepper. Combine tomato sauce, brown sugar, vinegar, soy sauce, and ginger. Pour over chicken and rice mixture. Bake, covered, in a 375° oven for 50 to 55 minutes or till the chicken is tender. Serves 8.

Can't decide on drumsticks or thighs? Use eight of each.

Come for Brunch

When you have a leisurely morning, combine breakfast
and lunch into a brunch. Reduce last-minute fuss
by selecting one of the recipes you can prepare the
night before. To complete the repast, add fresh fruit or
juice and toast.

Curried Shrimp Strata

1 **6-ounce package frozen peeled, cooked shrimp** ½ **of a 1-pound loaf of French bread, cubed (about 6 cups)** 1½ **cups shredded Swiss cheese (6 ounces)**	● Thaw shrimp. Drain well. In an 8x8x2-inch baking dish layer *half* of the bread cubes. Top with cheese and shrimp. Arrange remaining bread cubes on top.
4 **beaten eggs** 2¼ **cups milk** 1 **tablespoon curry powder** 2 **green onions, sliced** ½ **teaspoon salt** **Dash pepper**	● In a medium mixing bowl combine eggs, milk, curry powder, green onions, salt, and pepper. Pour over layers in dish. Cover and let stand for 1 hour at room temperature or chill overnight in the refrigerator. 　Bake, uncovered, in a 325° oven 50 to 55 minutes or till a knife inserted near the center comes out clean. Let stand 5 minutes before serving. Makes 6 servings.

To make our strata special, we added shrimp and a little curry powder.

Sausage and Sweet Potato Bake

1 20-ounce can pineapple
  chunks
1 18-ounce can sweet
  potatoes, drained and
  cut into ½-inch slices
1 pound fully cooked
  smoked sausage, cut into
  1-inch pieces
½ teaspoon finely shredded
  orange peel (set aside)
  Orange juice
4 teaspoons cornstarch
1 tablespoon prepared
  mustard

● Drain pineapple, reserving juice. In a 2-quart casserole combine pineapple, sweet potatoes, and sausage. Set aside.

For sauce, add enough orange juice to reserved pineapple juice to make 1 cup. In a small saucepan combine juice, orange peel, cornstarch, and mustard. Stir till smooth. Cook and stir over medium heat till thickened and bubbly. Pour over sausage mixture.

Bake, covered, in a 350° oven for 30 to 35 minutes or till heated through. Makes 4 servings.

For a quick brunch, try this stove-top method. Prepare the sauce in a large saucepan. Then, gently stir in the pineapple, potatoes, and sausage. Cover and cook over medium heat about 10 minutes or till hot, stirring occasionally.

Spinach-Egg Casseroles

2 tablespoons margarine *or*
  butter
2 tablespoons all-purpose
  flour
⅛ teaspoon pepper
1¼ cups milk
1 cup shredded American
  cheese (4 ounces)
1 10-ounce package frozen
  chopped spinach,
  thawed and well drained
½ cup chopped fully cooked
  ham

● In a medium saucepan melt the margarine or butter. Stir in flour and pepper till blended. Add milk all at once. Cook and stir over medium heat till mixture is thickened and bubbly. Add cheese. Cook and stir till cheese melts. Measure ¾ cup sauce and set aside. Stir spinach and ham into the remaining sauce in the saucepan.

For a head start on your brunch, cook the eggs the night before. Then, refrigerate them till morning.

4 hard-cooked eggs, cut in
  half lengthwise

● Divide spinach mixture evenly among four 10-ounce casseroles. Make an indentation in the center of the spinach mixture. Place two egg halves in each indentation. Top with reserved sauce.

Bake in a 350° oven for 15 to 20 minutes or till heated through. Serves 4.

Cheese and Egg Bake

¼ cup all-purpose flour
¼ cup margarine *or* butter, melted
⅛ teaspoon pepper

● In a large mixing bowl combine flour, margarine or butter, and pepper.

For a different twist, rinse and drain a 4½-ounce can of shrimp. Add it with the cottage cheese.

4 beaten eggs
1 cup cream-style cottage cheese, drained
1 cup shredded Monterey Jack cheese (4 ounces)
1 4-ounce can diced green chili peppers, drained
1 2-ounce jar diced pimiento, drained
2 slices bacon, crisp-cooked, drained, and crumbled
1 orange slice (optional)
Parsley sprigs (optional)

● Add eggs, cottage cheese, Monterey Jack cheese, chili peppers, and pimiento. Stir till combined. Pour mixture into a greased 10x6x2-inch baking dish.

Bake, uncovered, in a 375° oven for 25 to 30 minutes or till set and slightly puffed. Sprinkle with bacon. Garnish with orange slice and parsley, if desired. Makes 6 servings.

Baked Asparagus And Mushroom Omelet

1 cup fresh asparagus cut in 2-inch pieces *or* ½ of a 10-ounce package frozen cut asparagus
1 cup sliced fresh mushrooms
¼ cup sliced green onion

● Cook fresh asparagus, mushrooms, and green onion in a small amount of boiling water about 7 minutes or till tender. (Or, cook frozen asparagus, mushrooms, and green onion according to asparagus package directions.) Drain.

To keep your morning hassle free, mix up this easy oven omelet the night before. Then, cover and chill. Bake it the next morning as directed.

6 eggs
½ cup milk
¼ teaspoon salt
⅛ teaspoon ground nutmeg
⅛ teaspoon pepper
1 cup shredded process Swiss *or* Gruyère cheese (4 ounces)
2 tablespoons snipped parsley (optional)

● In a large mixing bowl combine eggs, milk, salt, nutmeg, and pepper. Beat with fork or rotary beater till blended. Stir in cooked vegetables and Swiss or Gruyère cheese. Turn egg mixture into a greased 10x6x2-inch baking dish.

Bake, uncovered, in a 375° oven for 20 to 25 minutes or till set. Sprinkle with snipped parsley, if desired. Serves 4.

Scrambled Egg Casserole

6 eggs
⅓ cup milk
  Dash pepper
2 tablespoons margarine
    or butter

● In a medium mixing bowl beat together eggs, milk, and pepper.

In a large skillet melt margarine or butter over medium heat. Add egg mixture. Cook without stirring till mixture begins to set on bottom and around edges. Using a large spoon or spatula, lift and fold partially cooked eggs so the uncooked portion flows underneath. Continue cooking over medium heat for 2 to 3 minutes or till eggs are firm but still moist. Turn into a greased 10x6x2-inch baking dish.

1 tablespoon margarine
    or butter
4 teaspoons all-purpose
    flour
¼ teaspoon paprika
¾ cup milk
¾ cup shredded American
    cheese (3 ounces)
¾ cup seasoned croutons

● In a small saucepan melt margarine or butter. Stir in flour and paprika. Add milk all at once. Cook and stir till thickened and bubbly. Add cheese. Stir till smooth. Pour over egg mixture.

Bake in a 375° oven for 12 to 15 minutes or till heated through. Sprinkle with croutons. Makes 4 servings.

Topped with croutons, this casserole tastes like scrambled eggs and toast in a dish. Just serve with juice and coffee.

Huevos con Frijoles

4 eggs
1 10¾-ounce can condensed
    cream of celery soup
1 8-ounce can red kidney
    beans, drained
1 4-ounce can diced green
    chili peppers, drained
2 green onions, sliced
2 tablespoons snipped
    parsley
⅛ teaspoon pepper
  Several dashes bottled hot
    pepper sauce
1½ cups shredded cheddar
    cheese (6 ounces)
  Taco sauce (optional)
  Dairy sour cream
    (optional)

● In a large mixing bowl beat eggs till blended. Stir in soup, kidney beans, chili peppers, green onions, parsley, pepper, and hot pepper sauce. Add cheese. Mix well. Pour mixture into a greased 8x8x2-inch baking dish.

Bake in a 350° oven for 30 to 35 minutes or till set. Let stand 5 minutes before serving. Top with taco sauce and sour cream, if desired. Makes 4 servings.

Honeydew melon or cantaloupe wedges perfectly complement this peppy dish.

Biscuit-Topped Chicken à la King

¼ cup chopped onion
2 tablespoons margarine
  or butter
3 tablespoons all-purpose
  flour
½ teaspoon poultry
  seasoning
¼ teaspoon salt
⅛ teaspoon pepper
1½ cups milk

● In a large saucepan cook onion in margarine or butter till tender. Stir in flour, poultry seasoning, salt, and pepper. Add milk all at once. Cook and stir till thickened and bubbly.

This classic is usually ladled over toast points or patty shells. But we topped ours with biscuits for one-dish convenience.

1½ cups chopped cooked
  chicken
1 cup frozen peas, thawed
1 2-ounce can mushroom
  stems and pieces,
  drained
2 tablespoons chopped
  pimiento
2 hard-cooked eggs,
  chopped

● Stir in chicken, peas, mushrooms, and pimiento. Cook till heated through. Gently stir in hard-cooked eggs. Turn mixture into a 1½-quart casserole. Bake in a 425° oven for 15 minutes.

1 package (6) refrigerated
  biscuits

● Cut each biscuit into quarters. Arrange biscuit quarters over chicken mixture. Bake in the 425° oven for 8 to 10 minutes more or till biscuits are golden. Makes 4 servings.

1 With a large spoon make six indentations in the turkey mixture. Make them large enough to hold an egg.

Turkey Hash

1 **medium onion, chopped**
   ($\frac{1}{2}$ cup)
2 **tablespoons margarine**
   or **butter**
2 **medium potatoes, cooked,**
   peeled, and chopped, *or*
   2 cups frozen hash
   browns, thawed
1$\frac{1}{2}$ **cups finely chopped fully**
   cooked smoked turkey
   breast
$\frac{1}{8}$ **teaspoon salt**
$\frac{1}{8}$ **teaspoon pepper**
$\frac{3}{4}$ **cup tomato juice**

● In a large skillet cook onion in margarine or butter till tender. Stir in potatoes, turkey, salt, and pepper. Spread in a greased 10x6x2-inch baking dish. Pour tomato juice over all. Bake in a 325° oven for 15 minutes.

6 **eggs**
$\frac{1}{4}$ **cup snipped parsley**
   (optional)

● Using the back of a spoon, make 6 indentations in turkey mixture. Break 1 egg into a small dish. Carefully slide the egg into an indentation. Repeat with remaining eggs. Bake about 20 minutes more or till the eggs are just set. Sprinkle with parsley, if desired. Makes 6 servings.

2 Carefully break an egg into a custard cup. Then, gently slip the egg from the custard cup into an indentation. Repeat with remaining eggs.

3 Return the casserole to the oven for 20 minutes or till the eggs are cooked just the way you like them. The whites should be set, and the yolks as firm or soft as you like.

Casseroles on the Side

Vegetables play a supporting role in main-dish casseroles,
but in side-dish casseroles, they're the star attraction.
All of these recipes feature a saucy vegetable or vegetable
combo baked in a dish. They taste delicious alongside meat,
fish, or poultry, and make great take-along dishes for
cookouts, picnics, and potlucks.

Swiss Scalloped Potatoes

1 **small onion, chopped** 3 **tablespoons margarine** *or* **butter** ¼ **cup all-purpose flour** ½ **teaspoon salt** ⅛ **teaspoon pepper** 2½ **cups milk** 6 **ounces sliced process** **Swiss cheese, torn** **(1½ cups)**	● For sauce, in a medium saucepan cook onion in margarine or butter till tender. Stir in flour, salt, and pepper. Add milk all at once. Cook and stir till thickened and bubbly. Add cheese. Cook and stir till melted. Remove from heat.
5 **medium potatoes, thinly** **sliced (5 cups)**	● Arrange *half* of the potatoes in a greased 2-quart casserole. Cover with *half* of the sauce. Repeat layers. Bake, covered, in a 350° oven for 1 hour. Stir. Bake, uncovered, about 30 minutes more or till potatoes are tender. Makes 8 servings.

**Make these taters to
tote. They're perfect for
a potluck dinner.**

Summer Squash Bake

4	cups sliced summer squash *or* zucchini (about 1 pound)
1	small onion, chopped

● In a large saucepan cook squash and onion in 1 cup boiling salted *water,* uncovered, for 5 minutes. Drain well.

1	7½-ounce can semicondensed cream of mushroom soup
½	of an 8-ounce container sour cream dip with toasted onion
½	cup shredded carrot
1	cup herb-seasoned stuffing mix
2	tablespoons margarine *or* butter, melted

● In a large mixing bowl combine soup, sour cream dip, and carrot. Fold in the squash mixture.

Toss stuffing mix and margarine or butter. In an 8x8x2-inch baking dish sprinkle ⅔ of the stuffing mixture. Spoon vegetable mixture over stuffing layer. Sprinkle remaining stuffing mixture around edges of the dish.

Bake, uncovered, in a 350° oven for 25 to 30 minutes or till heated through. Makes 6 servings.

Feature surplus summer squash or zucchini in this creamy casserole.

Baked Pinto Beans

¼	cup finely chopped onion
¼	cup finely chopped green pepper
1	teaspoon chili powder
1	clove garlic, minced
1	tablespoon margarine *or* butter
2	15-ounce cans pinto beans, drained
½	cup chunky salsa
½	cup shredded cheddar *or* Monterey Jack cheese (2 ounces)

● In a small skillet cook onion, green pepper, chili powder, and garlic in margarine or butter till vegetables are tender. Transfer to a 1½-quart casserole.

Stir in pinto beans and salsa. Bake, covered, in a 350° oven for 30 to 35 minutes or till heated through. Sprinkle with cheese. Makes 4 servings.

Fire up this dish by using cans of pinto beans with jalapeño peppers.

Summer Vegetable Bake

Summer Vegetable Bake

8 ounces fresh green beans, cut into 1-inch pieces (1½ cups), *or* one 9-ounce package frozen cut green beans
1 medium onion, chopped (½ cup)
1 10-ounce package frozen chopped spinach

● In a large saucepan bring 1 cup *water* to boiling. Add fresh beans and onion. Cover and simmer for 10 minutes. (For frozen beans, cook onion in the 1 cup boiling water for 5 minutes; add beans. Cook 5 minutes more.) Add spinach. Return to boiling. Simmer, covered, for 5 minutes more. Drain well.

1 tablespoon margarine *or* butter
1 tablespoon all-purpose flour
¼ teaspoon salt
¼ teaspoon garlic powder
Dash ground nutmeg
Dash pepper
⅔ cup milk
1 3-ounce package cream cheese, cut up

● Meanwhile, for sauce, in a small saucepan melt margarine or butter. Stir in flour, salt, garlic powder, nutmeg, and pepper. Add milk all at once. Cook and stir till thickened and bubbly. Add cream cheese. Stir till cheese is melted. Stir sauce into vegetable mixture. Turn into a 1-quart casserole.

½ cup soft bread crumbs
2 tablespoons grated Parmesan cheese
1 tablespoon margarine *or* butter, melted

● In a mixing bowl toss together bread crumbs, cheese, and margarine or butter. Sprinkle over vegetable mixture.
Bake, uncovered, in a 350° oven for 20 to 25 minutes or till heated through. Makes 6 servings.

Pictured at left.

This tasty green bean and spinach combo brings a smile to even the most somber faces (almost all of them, that is).

Sweet Potato Spoon Bread

1¼ cups milk
¼ cup thinly sliced green onion
½ cup yellow cornmeal

● In a medium saucepan stir milk and green onion into the cornmeal. Cook, stirring constantly, about 4 minutes or till the mixture is thick and pulls away from the sides of the pan. Remove from heat.

1 8-ounce can sweet potatoes, drained and mashed
1 tablespoon margarine *or* butter
½ teaspoon baking powder
½ teaspoon salt
2 egg yolks
2 egg whites
Grated Parmesan cheese
Margarine *or* butter

● Stir in mashed sweet potatoes, 1 tablespoon margarine or butter, baking powder, and salt. Beat in egg yolks.
Beat egg whites till stiff peaks form (tips stand straight). Gently fold beaten egg whites into yolk mixture. Turn mixture into a greased 1-quart casserole. Sprinkle with Parmesan cheese and dot with margarine or butter.
Bake in a 325° oven about 40 minutes or till a knife inserted near the center comes out clean. Serve with additional margarine. Makes 4 servings.

Although called a bread, it's more like a sweet potato soufflé. Actually, spoon bread is a quick bread that's soft enough to serve with a spoon. Try this one topped with margarine or butter.

Make-Ahead Mashed Potatoes

6 medium potatoes (about 2 pounds)	● Peel and quarter potatoes. Cook, covered, in boiling salted water for 20 to 25 minutes or till tender. Drain. Mash with a potato masher or beat with an electric mixer on low speed.	**Armed with this recipe, you avoid the last-minute rush of mashing potatoes.**
½ of an 8-ounce carton dairy sour cream 1 3-ounce package cream cheese, cut up 1 tablespoon margarine *or* butter 1 teaspoon onion salt ¼ teaspoon pepper ¼ to ½ cup milk 1 tablespoon margarine *or* butter	● Add sour cream, cream cheese, 1 tablespoon margarine, onion salt, and pepper. Gradually beat in enough of the milk to make smooth and fluffy. Turn into a greased 1½-quart casserole. Cover with foil. Chill up to 24 hours. To serve, dot with remaining margarine or butter. Bake, uncovered, in a 350° oven about 45 minutes or till heated through. Makes 6 servings.	
	Microwave Directions: In a 1½-quart microwave-safe casserole combine peeled and quartered potatoes and ½ cup *water*. Micro-cook, covered, on 100% power (high) for 15 to 20 minutes or till very tender, stirring once. Drain. Transfer potatoes to a large bowl. Mash potatoes and mix as above. Spoon into a greased 1½-quart casserole. Cover and chill up to 24 hours. Dot with remaining margarine. To serve, micro-cook, covered, on high for 8 to 10 minutes or till heated, stirring once.	

Eggplant Bake

1 beaten egg ¼ cup milk 1 medium eggplant (1 pound), peeled and cut into ¼-inch-thick slices 1 cup fine dry bread crumbs 2 tablespoons cooking oil	● Combine egg and milk. Dip eggplant slices in egg mixture, then in crumbs. In a 10-inch skillet cook slices, a few at a time, in hot oil over medium heat for 30 to 60 seconds per side, adding additional oil, if necessary. Arrange slices in a 12x7½x2-inch baking dish.	**We dressed up fried eggplant with a rich cheese and basil sauce.**
1 11-ounce can condensed cheddar cheese soup ½ cup milk ½ cup dairy sour cream 1 teaspoon dried basil, crushed ¼ teaspoon garlic powder ¼ teaspoon pepper	● Combine soup, milk, sour cream, basil, garlic powder, and pepper. Pour over eggplant. Bake, uncovered, in a 400° oven for 15 to 20 minutes or till heated. Makes 8 servings.	

Index

A-C

Baked Asparagus and Mushroom
  Omelet, 69
Baked Pinto Beans, 75
Basil Turkey with Rice, 55
Beef
  Beef and Bean Stew, 59
  Easy Oven Stew, 27
  Pepper and Beef Rolls, 28
Beef, cooked
  Beef Pot Pie, 46
  Oriental Beef Bake, 17
  Southern-Style Casserole, 50
Beef, ground
  Chili and Corn Bread Bake, 34
  Easy Ground Beef Pie, 39
  Fiesta Tamale Bake, 32
  Garden Beef and Rice Bake, 58
  Make-Ahead Lasagna Rolls, 55
  Meatball and Bean Stew, 49
  Meatball Pie, 39
  Mexicali Macaroni Pie, 41
  Pastitsio, 24
  Spaghetti Pie, 41
  Texas-Style Casserole, 61
  Transatlantic Pie, 42
Biscuit-Topped Chicken à la King, 71
Bratwurst Bake, Easy, 7
Brunswick Bake, 50
Cheese and Egg Bake, 68
Cheesy Rice Bake, 13
Chicken
  Brunswick Bake, 50
  Chicken and Green Beans
    Parmesan, 11
  Chicken and Rice in a Dish, 26
  Chicken Lasagna Rosettes, 52
  Coq au Vin, 27
  Curried Chicken Pilaf, 48
  Herbed Chicken and Rice, 34
  Orange Chicken with Rice, 10
  Spanish Chicken Casserole, 7
  Spicy Louisiana Chicken Bake, 21
  Sweet and Sour Drumsticks, 65
  Thanksgiving-in-a-Dish, 12
  Turkey Alfredo Casserole, 8
  Zippy Chicken Casserole, 62

Chicken, cooked
  Biscuit-Topped Chicken
    à la King, 71
  Chicken Chow Mein Bake, 20
  Chicken Enchiladas, 35
  Chicken Pot Pies, 46
  Chicken Stuffing Bake, 64
  Chicken Tetrazzini, 29
  Ham, Turkey, and Noodles, 60
  Havarti Chicken Bake, 6
  Mexican Turkey Casserole, 14
  Shortcut Chicken Manicotti, 36
  Thanksgiving-in-a-Dish, 12
  Turkey Alfredo Casserole, 8
  Zippy Chicken Casserole, 62
Chili and Corn Bread Bake, 34
Coq au Vin, 27
Corn Bread Topping, 34
Curried Chicken Pilaf, 48
Curried Shrimp Strata, 66

E-G

Easy Bratwurst Bake, 7
Easy Cheesy Fish Bake, 17
Easy Ground Beef Pie, 39
Easy Oven Stew, 27
Eggplant Bake, 78
Eggplant Pasta Casserole, 54
Eggs
  Baked Asparagus and Mushroom
    Omelet, 69
  Cheese and Egg Bake, 68
  Curried Shrimp Strata, 66
  Huevos con Frijoles, 70
  Scrambled Egg Casserole, 70
  Spinach-Egg Casseroles, 67
  Turkey Hash, 72
Fiesta Tamale Bake, 32
Fish
  Easy Cheesy Fish Bake, 17
  Flounder and Spinach Bake, 19
  Mom's Tuna-Noodle
    Casserole, 30
  Salmon and Artichoke Pie, 38
  Salmon Soufflé, 21
  Shrimp and Rice au Gratin, 16
  Tuna and Rice Casserole, 30

Fish *(continued)*
  Tuna-Spaghetti Casserole, 30
  Tuna-Spinach Noodle
    Casserole, 30
Flounder and Spinach Bake, 19
Garden Beef and Rice Bake, 58
Greek Pasta Pie, 41

H-K

Ham
  Ham and Broccoli Bake, 49
  Ham-It-Up Macaroni and
    Cheese, 75
  Ham, Turkey, and Noodles, 60
  Spinach-Egg Casseroles, 67
  Three-Bean and Ham Bake, 59
Havarti Chicken Bake, 6
Herbed Chicken and Rice, 34
Huevos con Frijoles, 70
Knockwurst, Apples, and
    Sauerkraut, 26

L-N

Lamb
  Greek Pasta Pie, 41
  Lamb-Vegetable Stew, 23
  Pastitsio, 24
Macaroni and Cheese, 24
Make-Ahead Lasagna Rolls, 55
Make-Ahead Mashed Potatoes, 78
Meatball and Bean Stew, 49
Meatball Pie, 39
Meatless main dishes
  Baked Asparagus and Mushroom
    Omelet, 69
  Cheesy Rice Bake, 13
  Eggplant Pasta Casserole, 54
  Huevos con Frijoles, 70
  Macaroni and Cheese, 24
  Scrambled Egg Cassserole, 70
Mexicali Macaroni Pie, 41
Mexican Turkey Casserole, 14
Microwave recipes
  Chicken and Green Beans
    Parmesan, 11
  Chicken Tetrazzini, 29
  Easy Bratwurst Bake, 7
  Fiesta Tamale Bake, 32

Microwave Recipes *(continued)*
  Flounder and Spinach Bake, 19
  Knockwurst, Apples, and
    Sauerkraut, 26
  Make-Ahead Mashed Potatoes, 78
  Mexican Turkey Casserole, 14
  Orange Chicken with Rice, 10
  Oriental Beef Bake, 17
  Shrimp and Rice au Gratin, 16
  Turkey Alfredo Casserole, 8
Mom's Tuna-Noodle Casserole, 30

O-P

Orange Chicken with Rice, 10
Oriental Beef Bake, 17
Pastitsio, 24
Pepper and Beef Rolls, 28
Pork
  Pork and Lentils, 33
  Pork Chop and Cabbage
    Dinner, 23
  Pork Chops with Scalloped
    Potatoes, 22
  Pork Pot Pie, 46
  Southern-Style Casserole, 50
  Tourtière, 45
Pot Pie Pastry, 39

S

Salmon
  Salmon and Artichoke Pie, 38
  Salmon-Potato Bake, 11
  Salmon Soufflé, 21
  Shrimp and Rice au Gratin, 16
Sausage
  Easy Bratwurst Bake, 7
  Fiesta Tamale Bake, 32
  Knockwurst, Apples, and
    Sauerkraut, 26
  Mexicali Macaroni Pie, 41
  Sausage and Sweet Potato,
    Bake, 67
  Sausage Twist Casserole, 51
  Spaghetti Pie, 41
  Spanish Seafood with Rice, 57
  Texas-Style Casserole, 61
  Upside-Down Pizza, 44
Savory Baked Eggplant, 78

Scrambled Egg Casserole, 70
Seafood
  Cheese and Egg Bake, 68
  Curried Shrimp Strata, 66
  Sherry-Sauced Scallops, 33
  Spanish Seafood with Rice, 57
Sherry-Sauced Scallops, 33
Shortcut Chicken Manicotti, 36
Shrimp
  Cheese and Egg Bake, 68
  Curried Shrimp Strata, 66
  Shrimp and Rice au Gratin, 16
  Spanish Seafood with Rice, 57
Southern-Style Casserole, 50
Spaghetti Pie, 41
Spanish Chicken Casserole, 7
Spanish Seafood with Rice, 57
Spicy Louisiana Chicken Bake, 21
Spinach-Egg Casseroles, 67
Summer Squash Bake, 75
Summer Vegetable Bake, 77
Sweet and Sour Drumsticks, 65
Sweet Potato Spoon Bread, 77
Swiss Scalloped Potatoes, 74

T-Z

Texas-Style Casserole, 61
Thanksgiving-in-a-Dish, 12
Three-Bean and Ham Bake, 59
Tourtière, 45
Tourtière Pastry, 45
Transatlantic Pie, 42
Tuna
  Mom's Tuna-Noodle
    Casserole, 30
  Tuna and Rice Casserole, 30
  Tuna-Spaghetti Casserole, 30
  Tuna-Spinach Noodle
    Casserole, 30
Turkey
  Basil Turkey with Rice, 55
  Chicken Pot Pies, 46
  Chicken Stuffing Bake, 64
  Chicken Tetrazzini, 29
  Chili and Corn Bread Bake, 34
  Easy Bratwurst Bake, 7
  Ham, Turkey, and Noodles, 60
  Havarti Chicken Bake, 6
  Mexican Turkey Casserole, 14

Turkey *(continued)*
  Sausage Twist Casserole, 51
  Shortcut Chicken Manicotti, 36
  Thanksgiving-in-a-Dish, 12
  Turkey Alfredo Casserole, 8
  Turkey and Broccoli Bake, 12
  Turkey Hash, 72
  Turkey Meatball Stew, 13
  Upside-Down Pizza, 44
  Zippy Chicken Casserole, 62
Turkey, cooked
  Chicken Stuffing Bake, 64
  Chicken Pot Pies, 46
  Chicken Tetrazzini, 29
  Ham, Turkey, and Noodles, 60
  Havarti Chicken Bake, 6
  Mexican Turkey Casserole, 14
  Shortcut Chicken Manicotti, 36
  Thanksgiving-in-a-Dish, 12
  Turkey Alfredo Casserole, 8
  Turkey and Broccoli Bake, 12
  Turkey Hash, 72
  Zippy Chicken Casserole, 62
Upside-Down Pizza, 44
Vegetables
  Baked Pinto Beans, 75
  Eggplant Bake, 78
  Make-Ahead Mashed Potatoes, 78
  Summer Squash Bake, 75
  Summer Vegetable Bake, 77
  Sweet Potato Spoon Bread, 77
  Swiss Scalloped Potatoes, 74
Zippy Chicken Casserole, 62

Tips

Attention, Microwave Owners, 16
Fast-Cooking Chicken, 64
Freezer Wraps, 56
If the Dish Fits . . . , 20
Serve It Hot! 60
Some Freezer Tips, 51